SOLEDAD
WOMEN

SOLEDAD WOMEN

Wives of Prisoners Speak Out

LORI B. GIRSHICK

PRAEGER

Westport, Connecticut
London

Library of Congress Cataloging-in-Publication Data

Girshick, Lori B.
   Soledad women : wives of prisoners speak out / Lori B. Girshick.
     p.   cm.
   Includes bibliographical references and index.
   ISBN 0-275-95409-9 (alk. paper)
   1. Prisoners' spouses—California—Soledad. 2. Prisoners—
California—Soledad—Family relationships. 3. Conjugal visits—
California—Soledad. 4. Soledad Correctional Training Facility.
I. Title.
HV8886.U5G57   1996
365'.6—dc20   95-45419

British Library Cataloguing in Publication Data is available.

Library of Congress Catalog Card Number: 95-45419
ISBN: 0-275-95409-9

First published in 1996

Praeger Publishers, 88 Post Road West, Westport, CT 06881
An imprint of Greenwood Publishing Group, Inc.

Printed in the United States of America

The paper used in this book complies with the
Permanent Paper Standard issued by the National
Information Standards Organization (Z39.48-1984).

10 9 8 7 6 5 4 3 2 1

This book is dedicated to the wives who show courage and strength as they support their husbands in prison.

Contents

Part III   Conclusion

Acknowledgments

This book represents the completion of a project dedicated to the women who participated. It reflects my commitment to reveal the impact on the lives of all women who struggle with the pain and challenge of loving someone in prison. I am indebted to their willingness to share with me.

Thank you to Liz Murphy, acquisition editor, Greenwood Publishing Group, for giving me this opportunity to share a neglected aspect of reality many would rather ignore. Her faith in this topic and in me is appreciated. Thank you also to Jean Lynch, Production Editor at Greenwood, for helping me to shape the finished product.

I want to thank Eve Spangler, who made this work possible. Without her continued support and faith in me over the years, I never would have reached my goal. Thanks also to Lynda Holmstrom, Severyn Bruyn, Seymour Leventman, and Ritchie Lowry for their input.

My friends were invaluable over these years of work. I want to especially thank Debbie Cipolla for her help, and Caroline Rose, whose feedback and encouragement helped me stay sane. Thanks also to Paula Alexander, Kathie Cutshall, Robert Polhemus, and Charlie Metzler for assistance and support. Special appreciation goes to Marielena Paniagua, who aided in the technical development of the manuscript.

SOLEDAD WOMEN

Prologue: I Leave in the Dark of Morning

I leave in the dark of morning, following the routine of the past year that dominates my life, creating at once a predictability and an arbitrariness to which I still cannot adjust. My thoughts wind their way from topic to topic, but the road ahead is straight. I am on Highway 101, heading south, and I am grateful for the simple path. Alone with my thoughts for two hours, I review, relive, and project conversations and situations past and yet to come. When I arrive at my destination, I will be locked up for the next twelve hours in a large, poorly ventilated, concrete-walled room with 200 other people.

We are the families and friends of prisoners at Soledad prison, different from each other in every way—social status, race, religion, political views, education, and life experience. What we have in common is caring about someone incarcerated in the state prison system. What brings me here draws them as well. When I leave, it will be nighttime, and I will have missed another warm and sunny day, driving home in the dark, alone with my thoughts again, on this straight stretch of Highway 101.

Today I'm wearing something new, a colorful jumpsuit. Clothing is about the only aspect of the visit that can vary, for the prisoners and the visiting room look the same day after day. I am conscious of the fact that the way I dress is a way for my husband to show me off, to be proud of something in his life in an environment with few other opportunities for pride. I can carry in only a small, plastic, see-through purse with some money for the vending machines (20 dollars maximum), a comb, and some photographs. Depending on the officers processing us, we may or may not bring in blank paper and a pen. No books other than Bibles, no magazines, no games to help pass the time. I hear that in some prison visiting rooms they have board games and card games available, but not here at Soledad. So the real variety is in what I wear and what we can think of to say in our hours together.

Of course, there are rules about visitors' clothing. We can't wear blue denim, since that's what prisoners wear, though we can wear blue dress pants. We can't wear skirts too short, or necklines too low in front or in back. No spaghetti strap dresses. I've heard you can't even wear a sleeveless top, but I've done it myself. I've seen a lot of miniskirts, and I've seen people turned away for gray denim, so it often depends on the officers on duty. This is one more issue about which we can be apprehensive. When I shop for clothes now, I always think in terms of the prison's rules. And I always bring a sweater just in case, for who knows when an officer might think something is too see-through or too low? It's not a comfortable feeling, being subjected to somebody's whim, but this is prison, and control, arbitrary or not, is what prison is all about.

I left early enough this morning to be one of the first people to be processed. Upon arrival, those of us going to Soledad-North go into the main building, called Central, take a number, and wait until 9 A.M. for the van to pick us up and take us to North. It's necessary to arrive at least an hour early to get a low number, but the waiting is worth it. If you have a higher number, you may miss the first van and have to wait another hour before even getting to processing. If it's cold, raining, or crowded, I wait in my car and think or read. More often, I stand around and talk to the other women.

Every drive down, I think about the problems with the numbers and the van. Sometimes the numbers aren't there yet or the van arrives late. Sometimes the officer driving the van doesn't go according to the numbers and visitors push their way on. Sometimes the fog is heavy, and for security reasons no van runs until the fog lifts sufficiently. Some days the fog isn't thick at all, but they do a fog count anyway to make sure no prisoners have escaped. This holds us up, and we visitors, mostly women and little children, stand waiting for the go-ahead. There are so many variables, I never know if my visit will start around 9:30, 10:30, or 11:00 A.M. I, like the other visitors, can have a short fuse when it comes to the delays. We have all gotten up early and driven far for our visit, and we want the maximum time with our loved ones.

I need to remember to ask my husband what he wants in his package. Four times a year we can send a box filled with approved of items, such as clothing, food, and cigarettes. The items must be factory sealed, and the clothes can only be in certain colors and styles. Shopping takes on a whole new meaning when items can be purchased only through catalogs or sent through the quarterly package. This gives us something to discuss and plan, and it's a willing contribution, albeit small, that I make toward his lifestyle. Even after I reconcile his desires with the prison limitations, he still ends up with the feeling it's Christmas. Breaking the boredom of canteen purchases, the food is especially welcome.

The occasional lost package or items that are confiscated for not fitting the specifications add to the antagonism between prisoners and guards. Because prisoners require a pass to pick up the package, and the hours to do so are limited, a longed-for package can sit in the office for days or weeks. It's one more issue of control.

Today will be like last week, and like next week as well. All we can do in there is sit in our seats, or walk around the room, or get something to eat from the vending machines. You can visit with other couples, but you're not supposed to spend too long at someone else's table. Officers usually tell you to move on. If you want a stretch break, to stand leaning against the wall and talk, an officer will come by and tell you to "get off the wall." It's not a comfortable or friendly environment, and there's a limit to how many times you can walk around the perimeter of the room. It's harder on the children. They can't run or jump or shout. They do get loud, and it's annoying, but without a place to play, it's very boring for the kids. Overall, it is a very controlled environment.

We could all use an outdoor area, but there isn't one. You need to stand on a chair (which isn't allowed) to look out the window, and the ventilation from these high windows seems nonexistent. By midmorning there's a cloud of cigarette smoke blanketing the room. You're engulfed in it, so you don't see it unless you walk around, and then you wonder how anyone can breathe in there. The smoke always gives me a headache that gets worse as the day wears on. I don't have any options except, of course, to end my visit and leave. Our first few hours together are the best, and as the smoke and boredom increase, we can get edgy with each other.

Some guards are friendly and don't watch the couples too closely. They let couples hug and kiss. We can almost feel normal. But others patrol the room, and confront a man if he has a hand on his wife's knee or if she has her head on his shoulder. A foot rub can be cause for a terminated visit. When these officers are present, it creates tension in the room, and we become preoccupied with the arbitrary power of the guards rather than with sharing our precious time together. Some officers are known for their hostile attitude toward prisoners' visitors and wives, yet they still staff the visiting room.

To me, the visits should be a time when we can comfort each other. Husbands and wives need affection, need to be held. We have problems with court cases, problems with money, and problems with our kids. We have bad news to sort through and communication problems like other couples. A husband and wife need to be able to relate to each other emotionally. The visiting room denies that need in spite of common sense telling us that the men would benefit from comforting and care, perhaps making their time inside less stressful.

Our only time of privacy comes during our conjugal, or family, visits. California is one of only 6 states that allow overnight visits between prisoners and their families on prison grounds. These visits give us time to strengthen our ties and remind us that we are a family. It's a much talked-about event between all husbands and wives. This is a time when I can bring in home cooking, books, magazines, and different clothes to wear. But the conditions of the trailers are pitiful, and I can only liken them to a slum. Furniture is broken and stained, the curtains are ripped. Sometimes the heating or the oven doesn't work. These conditions add to the feelings that we are worthless people. It's difficult to reconcile feeling grateful with feeling very uncomfortable. I don't expect a palace, but I truly would appreciate a cleaner environment, with furnishings and cookware in better condition.

Conjugal visits happen every three months for us, since we are on the scheduled list rather than the standby list. Standby families can be called on a moment's notice due to a cancellation or a no-show, and they can have visits as frequently as every month. My work schedule doesn't permit such flexibility, so we accept our four times a year when we aren't under the watchful eyes of others.

It's usually the same early crowd of visitors, and it didn't take me long to learn that most of the information about visiting rules or what's going on in the prison comes from the wives. We learn more from each other than from the officers or the paperwork. It's the women who are sensitive to the long waits, arbitrary rules, communication problems, dress codes, family visit concerns, and worries about lockdowns and riots. We understand through our shared experience, our shared degradation, that we need to help one another with information, rides, and encouragement.

These women are my friends, and they understand my marriage more than my own family or my other friends. There is the shared perception that only a prisoner's wife can understand another prisoner's wife. You have to be in the situation to appreciate what we go through. What would we do without each other? How could we bear the isolation in the outside world? Visits are the "real world," while time outside the prison is just the time in between visits.

When I got married, no one I worked with knew about it. I took a day off "to take care of personal business." I felt I couldn't tell anyone because I feared their reaction. No shared joy, no congratulations, no wedding gifts. I don't wear my wedding ring except when I'm at the prison, because that's where I feel most like a married woman. One of my coworkers married a month earlier than I did, and such a fuss was made! I admit it, I was envious. Not so much of her fancy wedding plans and parties, but of the openness, the excitement. I missed the same honesty. By now I've told a few people at work. We don't talk about it much; they don't ask me how my weekend was. I think they don't know what to ask or say, and don't want to say something negative or offensive. Prisoners are simply not a very popular group.

The morning sky is changing to pale pink and orange. This is my favorite part of the drive, when the lightness seeps into the black that had enveloped me and reminds me of those glimmers of happiness my weekends bring. I see my surroundings: farmland, migrant workers, and some small towns. My thoughts become more focused on my visit. I picture myself waiting at the door my husband will walk through, and feeling the thrill as he sweeps me into his arms. There is that one precious moment that we've waited for all week, that one instant we feel completely alone and private. Then we turn around, check in with the guards, and take our seats.

I have many fears and worries. Has there been another racial incident during the week? Will they be on lockdown and have to be escorted individually to the visiting room, delaying our visit? Will there be a car search of the visitors? I've learned to detect problems by the activity near the prison entrance. If there are officers at the front, there's a car search or there was a recent escape. If it's a car search, we could be delayed for hours. Everything is emptied out of the car, and dogs jump in to sniff for drugs. We women stand and wait.

It's humiliating, this presumed guilt by association because you care for someone inside. The impression I get most often is that guards feel we women have broken some law, that we obviously are lower class, that we are suspect. Well, I suppose it's no surprise. I am suspicious of the guards, and dread their control and attempts at humiliation. I do my best to be friendly, yet they are in the oppositional role of the enemy. It's a two-way street of dislike, and it is not pleasant.

We prisoners' wives lead a double life. Nowhere are we free, not within the prison walls with our husbands, not outside in the free society. I can only shake my head in wonder as to how we survive it all — the emotional and financial burdens, stress on our marriages, and undermining of our self-esteem.

Well, here I am, here's my exit off the highway. Like most prisons, Soledad is its own isolated kingdom, looking completely out of place in the countryside. I don't see any activity at the gate, and I'm relieved. There are at least a few problems I won't have to deal with today. There's no fog, more good fortune. I park my car, walk toward the prison, see my friends, and wave. I'm home for the next 12 hours, living out my married life within the boundaries of the prison walls — knowing that love can unlock at least one door.

Part I

INTRODUCTION

Chapter 1

Why Study Wives of Prisoners?

Several years ago I invited a deputy district attorney (DA) to speak to a Law and Society class I taught at a local community college. As we talked before class, I mentioned that I was conducting research on wives of prisoners. He shook his head and said, "Oh, that must be interesting. It's hard to understand how they go through all that. And those women who marry inmates who are already in, have you spoken to many of them?" "Yes," I replied, "it's not uncommon." "Don't you think there's something wrong with that? I mean, are these women pathological?" he asked. "Not at all," I answered. "They marry men on the inside [who are incarcerated] for the same reasons people on the outside marry each other with their own particular set of problems."

What this DA did not realize was that at that time I was married to a prisoner whom I had met on the inside. Here he was, implying that I had a problem, a pathology, because I had fallen in love with a man convicted of a crime, and had married him. I did not take the comment personally, but I doubt he would have said that about me had he known of my marriage. After all, I was a professional, attractive woman, and did not fit the image of prisoner's wife. This DA displayed the widespread public perception of wives of prisoners: they are seen as guilty by association, and they are seen as losers. This perception affects policy decisions, on the one hand, and how the women view themselves, on the other.

THE CRIMINAL AS "OTHER"

There are few aspects of life that grip us like criminal behavior. The terms "criminal" and "victim" immediately evoke emotions that have been influenced through mass media portrayals of crime or through personal experience. The impersonal, unpredictable reality of crime frightens and alarms us. We know that the criminal is bad, perhaps even crazy; definitely he or she is different from us, having forfeited the claims to human decency through his or her actions. Criminals have not obeyed the rules; they have broken the bounds of predictability.

The saturation of news coverage of criminals rarely reveals the troubled childhoods, poor work histories, broken families, or drug and alcohol abuse that exist in the majority of cases. To connect with these personal factors would be too humane. It is more comfortable for the public at large to view the criminal as asocial, without a stake in society, one who has nothing to lose by his or her criminal activity. We prefer to think of them as the "other," devoid of feelings, hopes, or dreams that we ourselves may hold. We refuse to connect with them emotionally—except in outrage. In addition, Irwin (1980) writes, the view that those convicted of crimes are monsters is self-serving for prison bureaucrats and elected officials, who protect their jobs and divert attention away from white-collar crimes.

The victim is frequently blameless, perhaps a wife or a child, a neighbor, or a complete stranger. We shake our heads in sympathy and in fear, with the knowledge that it could have been us. We want to punish the offender, both to avenge the unfortunate victim and to protect ourselves. The criminal appears completely evil and has none of our sympathy.

The victim should have our sympathy, and the offender should be punished. But there are other persons involved besides the criminal and the victim who are affected by the criminal actions, people who rarely make the media spotlight. The families of the victims bear the emotional and financial impact of whatever consequence the victim faces. Perhaps it is adjusting to disability, compensating for financial loss, coping with fear and insecurity, or grieving the death of the victim.

The families of the offenders bear the emotional and financial impact of incarceration of their loved one. Unlike the victims' families, the prisoners' families are not viewed with sympathy or compassion. Rather, they are viewed as suspect, perhaps as equally guilty of the crime, due to their relationship to the offender. Yet the lives of these wives, children, and parents are dramatically changed due to the prisoner's behavior. The adjustment they must make, under the most difficult odds, is rarely portrayed in the news or understood by the public. Most of the public rarely gives them a thought one way or another, for to acknowledge these relationships would be to admit that criminals can have loving relationships, feelings for others, and dreams for their children. Even harder, it would mean acknowledging that others care about and love them. We find it hard to believe that the criminal has these human emotions or is the recipient of them.

FAMILY DISMEMBERMENT

Loss of a family member through incarceration is different from loss through separation by other means. Some separations have social approval; others do not. When a spouse dies, people offer sympathy and help; a divorce might indicate failure or bad judgment (Weiss, 1979). But, as Fishman and Cassin (1981, p. 6) point out, "Unlike death, the absent member will eventually return; unlike divorce, hospitalization, or military service, there is a social stigma attached to the offender's incarceration."

According to OPEN, Inc., an educational center for offenders and their families, the sense of loss is *the* central experience of the family when a family member is incarcerated. The losses that must be grieved include emotional and financial supports, and the roles that person played, as well as that person's physical presence (Rollo & Adams, 1987). Yet, as Fishman (1990) points out, the public at large views incarceration as something that was asked for, not as a loss.

When parents are in prison, their attachment to their children is broken. Lowenstein (1986) points out that separation due to incarceration is especially unique in its effects on children because of the stigma attached to it. Further, Lowenstein points out that these households are temporarily single-parent, as opposed to permanently single-parent. This makes the situation of these families closer to that of families in which there is hospitalization, chronic illness, or separation due to military duty (Rosenfeld & Rosenstein, 1973). The wife functions as a single parent, sharing custody of the children with an absentee father (Koenig, 1985).

Since prison populations are disproportionately poor and minority, the lack of concern and planning for the families of prisoners reflects a particular disregard for the impact of incarceration upon the well-being of prisoners' children (Hinds, 1980). These are the families with the fewest resources and the least political clout. Prisoners' wives and children are sometimes called the "forgotten victims of crime" as they try to adjust to the consequences of a crime they didn't commit. Smith (1987, p. AA1) reports in the *Sacramento Bee* that those who try to keep their families together may pay the price of "poverty, stress-related health problems and, sometimes the hardest to bear, social ostracism. . . . As one wife put it, 'People look at him as a criminal. They look at me as something lower.'"

According to Flanagan and Jamieson (1988), almost half of all male prisoners have been married, and about one-fourth of the total inmate population is currently married. We don't have the exact number of how many family members are affected by the current incarceration of more than 110,000 people in California. Executive Director Peter Breen of Centerforce, a prisoner family advocacy agency, estimates there are perhaps 750,000 affected family members (interview, April 17, 1991). And consider this: by 1971, when the number of U.S. casualties of the Vietnam war reached 58,000, 30,000 widows and orphans, 80,000 parents, 60,000 grandparents, and approximately 80,000 brothers and sisters—at least 250,000 Americans—had experienced the loss of an immediate family member (McCubbin & Dahl, 1976). Incarceration of a family member affects a significant portion of the population.

WHY STUDY FAMILIES OF PRISONERS?

This research highlights the impact of incarceration of the male prisoner on the "free" family. The focus here is on the wives (or girlfriends) and secondarily on the children of these men. I seek to explore the distinctive experience of these women to contribute to social theory and research. Researching women's perspectives is necessary because women's experience has been omitted, trivialized, or suppressed in dominant research (Anderson et al., 1990; Millman & Kanter, 1975; D. E. Smith, 1987).

Furthermore, Hartsock (1983) describes standpoint epistemology as knowing from the point of view of those in the disadvantaged position. In this case, the disadvantaged position is the women's link with convicted criminals. Prisoners' wives live both in the world outside the prison and within the prison system. They have a more complete view of social reality because they experience the dominant culture's perspective of prisoners and prisons in addition to the impact on their lives by the prison system. They are more knowledgeable about the impact of the prison system on their lives than anyone else. Hooks (1984) speaks similarly of blacks who operate in the dominant white world, yet also know the black subculture.

With imprisonment of the husband/father, family and marital roles become confused and undergo change. New roles must be established. I explore how prison affects the stability of an intimate relationship, the financial impact on the family trying to maintain the man on the inside and themselves on the outside, the interactions between the women and the prison system, the women's views on rehabilitation, and the criminal justice system's response to prisoners' families. There are virtually no studies on the impact of incarceration on the husband/father. This area clearly needs further study.

In his 1976 study of prisoners' families, Schneller argues that classical penologist Cesare Beccaria's notion of the "principle of specificity" was violated. This principle states that no one except the convicted criminal should be punished for his crime. Koenig (1985, p. 104) similarly finds in her study that despite the intention to punish only the offender, "wives of offenders become unfortunate victims of crime, as their lives are adversely affected by the offender's sentence." In fact, Fishman (1990) points out that it is the women who must deal with the men's problems. When the men are incarcerated, the women deal with the courts, the lawyers, the prison; they suffer stigmatization and other effects on their families. She views the impact as two separate but parallel sets of experiences: those of the prisoner and those of the wife, with the wife's experience based on his situation. These women are also doing time. While the husband does not have to worry about food, clothing, or housing, the wife has to cope with the bills, the children, visiting at the prison, and so forth. "'Punishment' was being on the outside and having to cope with the business of living" (Fishman, 1990, p. x).

There are several compelling reasons to study these families. From a criminal justice perspective, studies have shown that the family is a strong rehabilitation agent. Prisoners who maintain positive contact with their families show less recidivism. A 1972 California Department of Corrections study by Holt and Miller found that only 50 percent of the "no contact" prisoners completed one year of parole without arrest, whereas 70 percent of prisoners who had three visitors were arrest-free in one year. "Loners" were six times more likely to end up back in prison in their first year out. Holt and Miller argue that the family should be viewed as the prime rehabilitative agent.

A New York study (MacDonald, 1980) had a similar argument when it found that the recidivism rate of the program participants was 67 percent less than the expected number. In Massachusetts, similar findings were revealed in a 1985 study that examined correctional programs fostering societal links related to family, jobs, and social roles (LeClair, 1985). Criminal justice systems are concerned with costs, safety, and security. If fewer prisoners circulate through the system due to increased family unity, costs are cut. Family visits are an essentially free resource, as the families bear the burden of travel, food, and lodging needed during visiting. The cost of personnel to supervise visiting programs is certainly less than the costs of processing and housing more prisoners.

From a sociological perspective, the family is the most basic unit of society. The family unit is a primary relationship that provides opportunities for support, security, well-being, a sense of worth, and carrying out social roles. Without primary group affiliation, individuals feel rootless, despairing, and a sense of anomie (Weiss, 1974a). When prisoners' families undergo some of the worst stresses in attempting to maintain that unit, sociologists need to be concerned about the impact of these hardships.

Epps (1982) points out that crime is more than a problem between an individual and the state; it is also a problem of broken relationships. As Breen said in an interview (April 17, 1991), "The family is the basic unit of society, and in order to sustain society we need to put it back together." The criminal justice system should not act without knowing the status of the prisoner's family during sentencing, housing assignment, transfer, and so forth. The family, as the focal point of human relationships, bears the consequences of criminal justice policy that ignores the reality of family ties to the prisoner. At some point, these two systems need to work together for mutual benefit. According to Kaplan et al. (1977), social networks, among prisoners' families and the agencies that assist them, can help prisoners and their families deal with stress, health care needs, practical aid, and information. Social networks can bridge the gap between life on the inside and life on the outside.

Another sociological aspect to be developed in this research is the focus on women's roles in relationship maintenance. Women are socialized to be other-oriented and to be emotional caretakers. Lester (1982, p. 453) argues, "As a result of the socialization process, both men and women assume different roles in behavior, goals, self-images, and life experiences. Women are often considered to be the second sex and are therefore expected to define themselves through relationships with father, husband, or children." Furthermore, some social psychologists argue that caring and nurturing define both the identity and the activity of women (Chodorow, 1978; Gilligan, 1982; Miller, 1986).

This study examines how women maintain the family while the man is in prison, while the reverse does not hold when the female is incarcerated. For example, Carlson and Cervera (1991) state that how the wife adjusts to the incarceration may determine whether the relationship lasts–and whether the offender has a stable family to come home to, contributing to lower recidivism. However, men do not support women who are incarcerated, they rarely visit, and there is no expectation that men will keep the family together on the outside. According to Vaux (1985), gender may be the most important dimension of social status in social support interactions.

The perspective of the public is another major reason to study prisoners' families. A concern with crime cannot be detached from a concern with increasing incarceration rates. During the time this study was conducted (1985–86), there were 50,000 prisoners incarcerated in California. Approximately 48 percent were convicted of property crimes, 26 percent convicted of violent crimes, 11 percent convicted of drug offenses, 6 percent convicted of sex offenses, and 9 percent convicted of other offenses. Today there are approximately 110,000 people incarcerated in California. Forty-three percent of them committed violent offenses; 27 percent, property offenses; 24 percent, drug offenses; and 6 percent, other offenses.

The punishment approach to crime has not worked in California. Even the Blue Ribbon Commission on Inmate Population Management appointed by conservative former Governor George Deukmejian found in its 1990 Final Report that the criminal justice system was "out of balance." It called for more intermediary steps before incarceration, primarily those that would be community-based. One step toward establishing these options includes giving the families of prisoners the opportunity to strengthen their family units.

HOW THE STUDY BEGAN

In January 1985, I began a correspondence with a prisoner at Soledad. We met, and married in August of that year. I knew I was entering hardship and disapproval. I began a secret life, in which most people who knew me didn't know of my marriage, not uncommon among wives of prisoners. Through my weekly visits to my husband, I met many other prisoners' wives, and it was through them that I learned how to adjust to the prison system. They became not only my source of information but also my source of support. No one outside the situation can truly understand this system that is filled with heartbreak and degradations.

As a sociologist, the bonding of the women was so striking to me that I began mulling over the idea of writing a book about their experiences told through their eyes. As a prisoner's wife, I was already a participant-observer and had insight into this unique world. I wrote an interview format with broad questions relating to the experience of women visiting at the prison and the impact on their personal lives of being married to a prisoner. In January 1986 I began in-depth interviews with 25 other prisoners' wives (some were steady girlfriends at the time of interview). I also began to tape-record my own feelings about my visits, my relationship, and the study I had undertaken. A reflection on my own experience is given in Appendix C.

In her opening remarks at a January 25, 1992 symposium at Stanford University on "The Resilient Woman: Strength in the Face of Adversity," Carol Gilligan stated that "empirical" means "experienced." Everywhere that women communicate with each other presents us with empirical evidence, which needs to be included in what we know. Women's voices, for so long omitted from scientific research, need to be heard.

The method a researcher uses determines what counts as evidence and what will be used as verification (MacKinnon, 1989). "Method," according to Shanley and Schuck (1975, p. 633), "is not neutral; it establishes the criteria by which one judges the validity of conclusions, and consequently carries with it not simply technical skills but deeper philosophical commitments and implications." Feminist methodology is not so much a methodology, but a feminist perspective on the research process (Taylor & Rupp, 1991). Bunch (1979, p. 9) writes: "Feminism is an entire world view or *gestalt*, not just a laundry list of 'women's issues.'"

Nielsen (1990) writes of the challenge to the scientific method as the ultimate test of knowledge. Feminist research questions the basic assumption that objectivity is necessary, desirable, and even possible (Fee, 1983). The researcher is in a socially defined position, and cannot be devoid of perspective (Acker et al., 1991).

Feminist researchers try to reduce the power difference between themselves and those they research (Fonow & Cook, 1991). This is accomplished through the research methods chosen and the researcher's view of her own role in the research process. Oakley (1981) attempts a nonhierarchical process in which the researcher invests some of herself in the research relationship. In her study of new mothers, for example, she responded to questions asked of her, as she had been a new mother, and shared her own experience with her subjects. Further, Oakley feels that making an interview an interactional exchange reduces the objectification of the subject as data. Interactive interviewing personalizes and humanizes the researcher and puts the interviewee and researcher on a more equal footing. In D. E. Smith's study of mothers and their interaction with their children's schooling, the interviewers were themselves single mothers who participated in their own children's schooling. They therefore could speak with knowledge of the school organization, of "knowing *how* rather than knowing *that*" (1987, pp. 188–89).

The women in this study were willing to talk to me primarily because they trusted I would understand what they were going through. They also believed that getting this information out to the public might make a difference in lessening the stigma of the prisoner's family. Many of them were excited to participate in a study, something outside their ordinary experience. As one of them, they accepted that I understood what they were talking about and that I was able to describe and translate their experiences accurately. These women speak out through this research in the hope that you will hear them.

DESIGN OF THE STUDY

This study employs both participant-observation and in-depth interviewing. It uses what D. E. Smith (1987, p. 46) calls "the everyday world as problematic." The interview questionnaire I developed covers the areas most affected by marriage to a prisoner, tapping where the women actually were and how their everyday worlds were put together. I hoped to give the women voice, and this voice needs to be placed in the context of the "relations of ruling"—the external power and regulation that structure their lives. This external structure includes the criminal justice system, which perceives its needs as quite different from the needs of the women. The compelling forces of that system incorporate the politics of punishment, the dynamics of classism and racism, and the notion of stigma.

The everyday world is shaped by processes beyond the individual's experience and by the interrelations of many such experienced worlds (D. E. Smith, 1987, p. 134). When using the method of institutional ethnography, D. E. Smith begins with the daily lives of women and moves from there to examine how their activities are played out in organizational processes. For example, in one study Smith asked women how they organized their lives in relation to their children's schooling. Next she interviewed school administrators and teachers. "Our strategy would move from particular experiences to their embedding in the generalizing social organization of the school" (D. E. Smith, 1987, p. 183). She could look from the perspective of the mothers out onto the school system. I attempt to duplicate this method by first exploring the wives' perspectives of their lives and then looking at the prison system.

After the standard demographic information about the prisoner and the wife (age, race, education, religion), I also asked about conviction, sentence length, time already served, how the couple met, and if they had children. In open-ended questions, I asked about economic impact, relationship impact, family reaction, support network, dealing with the prison system, impact on children, coping with the ongoing situation, rehabilitation, and hopes and dreams. The interviews, which took from one to three hours, were taped and later transcribed. The interview format is reproduced in Appendix A.

I recruited the 25 women in a variety of ways, using primarily a snowball method. First, I asked those women I had become acquainted with to participate. Most readily agreed; a few first asked their husbands. Second, through word of mouth I was introduced to other women I might have seen but hadn't met. In addition, I posted notices about my study at the Friends Outside hospitality house in Salinas, and I put a notice in the Prisoner's Rights Union's *Resource*

Guide. The notice at the hospitality house brought me one woman, while the *Resource Guide* listing brought me many letters from prisoners asking about the study, but no wives to interview.

While my sample does include a range of ages, a racial mix, an educational span, and women from poor to well-to-do social classes, it is not scientific. However, I am not trying to generalize from the 25 women to a larger population. Instead, I am exploring how the institutional practices of the prison system organize the experiences of these individual women as wives of prisoners (D. E. Smith, 1987).

In many cases, the women and I grew closer after the interview. We had more to talk about because they were very interested in the project. Prior to the interviews, I had known nine of the women casually and I was friendly with nine others (meaning we talked regularly about our situation while waiting to visit). I met seven of the women because of the study. I never met sixteen of the husbands. I had been introduced to three of the husbands but had never spoken with them, and six of the husbands, I had spoken to, basically because they were friends of my husband. This revealed several points to me related to race. The women interacted regardless of race. When we spoke to one another before a visit, race was not a factor. The men, however, had a strict racial attitude in their conduct. Visiting room etiquette reflected what was going on within the prison. They rarely mixed racially, though the mixed couples (generally black husband, white wife) tended to socialize most with other mixed couples and black couples. Thus, once the men arrived for the visit, much of the mixed-race socializing of the women ended. Some of the husbands objected to the wives' participation in the study and would not speak to me because I was in a mixed marriage. That is part of the reason why I did not meet them. Some of the husbands were in a different section of the Soledad facility, so I never had an opportunity to meet them.

The interviews took place between January and August 1986. I spoke with 15 of the women in their homes (in King City, Oakland, Alameda, Redwood City, Morgan Hill, San Jose, Salinas, and the town of Soledad). One interview was in my home, one in my car in the Soledad prison parking lot before visiting, three at a restaurant near the prison, and four took place in motel rooms near the prison. One interview was sent in by mail.

I conducted four-month, eight-month, and one-year follow-ups to each interview. These results are reported in Appendix B.

The open-ended interview format allowed me to probe for greater clarification, go in directions not initially expected, and permitted the women to speak their minds. When a woman would ask me about my experiences, I answered briefly. There were distractions and noise in the restaurant, and in the homes, children often would interrupt or the phone would ring. These seemed minor problems.

A greater discomfort with the interview method is knowing that respondents may not always tell a full story or have not told the truth. After all, people do not want to look bad to others, including researchers. I had made up my mind to accept fully what the women told me as their perception, but in a few cases I knew of contradictory information. While this made me uneasy, I still feel confident that this method captures more of the complete truth, even with some inconsistencies, than any other methodology would allow.

Inconsistencies in themselves do not invalidate the research. Oakley (1974a) found in her in-depth interviews of 40 housewives on the topic of housework that direct statements sometimes seemed contradictory. Oakley writes, "Listen carefully to what women say" (1974a, p. 103), because housework is such a personal subject for the women and their identity is tied to it. She felt the true views of the women would be revealed in their indirect commentaries. Vaughan (1986), in her study of relationships that broke up, adds that people were selective in what they told her due to a need for privacy and in order to save face. She also felt that she did not have to know all their secrets in order to capture how relationships ended.

DESCRIPTION OF PARTICIPANTS AND THEIR SPOUSES

More women (10) were in their thirties than any other age category. One woman was 19, and one was 53. Eight women were in their twenties, and five were in their forties. Most of the women (17) were white. There were five black women, one Puerto Rican, one Filipino-Mexican, and one Mexican-American. The women were fairly well educated. Only two did not complete high school. Ten graduated from high school or had a General Equivalency Diploma (GED). Fourteen women had some college, and of those, there was one with a nursing degree, three with a bachelor's degree, and one with a Ph.D. In addition, three women had some vocational training (medical assistant, hotel and restaurant management, modeling school, travel agent training).

Only two women had no religious affiliation. The breakdown for the others was as follows: Baptist (six), Catholic (four), Christian (three), Protestant (three), Pentecostal (two), Methodist (one), Lutheran (one), Christian Scientist (one), Jehovah's Witness (one), and Jewish (one).

More prisoners (12) were in their thirties than any other age. Nine men were in their twenties, three were in their forties, and one was 51. Fourteen prisoners were white, nine were black, there was one Mexican-American, and one Mexican. Examining the racial composition of marriages, we find six mixed marriages, or 24 percent.

The men were not as well educated as the women. Four of them had dropped out of high school. Twelve had a high school diploma or GED. Nine had some college, including one with an A.A. degree and one with a bachelor's degree. The men's religious affiliation varied slightly from that of the women. Four had no preference. There were six Baptists, six Catholics, five Protestants, two Christians, one Pentecostal, and one agnostic.

When we look at the crime or crimes the men were convicted of, there were more violent offenses than any other category. This was not representative of the prison population as a whole at the time of the study. Due to multiple charges, these numbers add up to more than 25. There were 15 violent offenses, which include assault, rape, and murder. Four men were charged with drug-related crimes, nine with property-related crimes, and there were three parole violations. Three wives preferred not to reveal the crime(s) their husbands were convicted of, and one wife was not sure of the major crime (in addition to his parole violation). Judging by the sentence lengths, these were likely to have been violent offenses.

Eleven men had sentence lengths of one to eight years. Nine men were facing sentences of 10 to 21 years. Of these, five faced 10 to 13 years, and four faced 16 to 21 years. Five men had life sentences. One man had an additional five-year federal sentence to serve when he was released from state prison.

More than half the men (14) had served a minimum of two years at the time of the study. Just under half (11) had served between two and seven years. Seven years was the longest any prisoner in the sample had served. Eight men had served between four and seven years.

Almost all of the women (21) knew their husbands before they entered prison. Of these, eight had been married before the prison term, 12 got married after sentencing or after the incarceration started, and one married shortly after the time of the interview. Four women met their husbands through correspondences. Of these, two got married during the incarceration, and two were not yet married at the time of the interview. It is very interesting to note how many women marry the men after they begin their prison sentence in order to pursue their relationships seriously.

Twelve of the 25 couples had children, including one couple expecting their first child. There were 29 children altogether. The children were almost all young. Two families had six children each: one where ages ranged from 9 to 19, and one where the ages ranged from 14 to 20. Of the 17 other children, nine were five and under, and eight were seven to 13.

I have made a conscious decision to refer to the incarcerated men as "prisoners" rather than "inmates" or "convicts". Since they are wards of a prison, this seems the most accurate term. I also refer to the guards as guards rather than use the euphemism "correctional officer". Their job is to watch over or guard the prisoners, so "guard" is the most accurate term. While the women were not all married at the time of interview, I refer to them all as "prisoners' wives" because they either were planning to marry or were very serious girlfriends. Also, the women are referred to by first name only, and in some cases that name is a pseudonym. For the purposes of retaining anonymity, the men are referred to only by the first letter of their names. First initials are also used for children, and initials for the names of lawyers or other administrators.

The women in this study are committed to maintaining and stabilizing a family for the prisoner and their children. They do not have the profile of losers, yet they face the stigma of their outcast prisoner husbands. These women marry their husbands for the same reasons that women on the outside marry free men— love, attraction, interests, understanding, acceptance. They also have relationship problems similar to relationships on the outside—jealousies, lack of communication, sexual problems, emotional distancing. However, when you add the unique differences of these marriages, the women do face challenges that result in different needs and sacrifices. Their situation cries out for greater support and validation in the society for their efforts to retain a valued and worthy family unit—a family in which the man is in prison and will one day be reunited with them.

CHAPTER OVERVIEW

Chapter 2, "Families and Incarceration," examines the difference between male and female incarceration and male and female gender role socialization around caring behavior, explores family separation factors, reviews the literature on prisoners and families, and looks at the importance of carrying out family roles.

Chapter 3, "Living with Secrets," discusses the secret life wives of prisoners frequently live, the stigma they experience, how family and friends react to their husbands' incarceration, and who they tell about their marriages.

"Relationship Realities," Chapter 4, examines how their relationships are affected, from communication issues to jealousy to attempts to carry out family roles. Also discussed is the impact of their fathers' imprisonment on the children.

Chapter 5, "Family Finances," discusses the cost of incarceration of a family member to the family. These costs include visiting, phone calls, packages, family visiting, and housing for the "free" family.

Chapter 6, "Visiting at the Prison," delves into how the wives feel about the visiting room conditions, visiting rules, the guards, their need for information, family visiting, and stress over visiting.

"Dealing with the System," Chapter 7, gives the wives' views on the many problems they encounter with this system that has such control over their lives. These issues range from car searches to family visiting problems to loss of visiting privileges to the worry they have for their husbands' well-being.

"The Role of the Family," Chapter 8, explores how the wives feel about their roles in their husbands' rehabilitation and how they evaluate what the prison system is doing with their husbands. Also examined is their view of the role of public attitudes toward prisoners.

The concluding chapters, 9 and 10, discuss policy recommendations and programs that are pro-family and would be beneficial both for the families and for society. The family is taken as a key rehabilitative agent. Final comments are then made about wives as caretakers and point to three primary themes.

This is not my personal story. My husband and I filed for divorce in 1987, the marriage falling victim to the stress of the prison system, abuse, and more common relationship problems. In spite of my own divorce, I have never wavered in my support regarding the hardship these men and women experience in their attempts to maintain their families. This is the story of 25 prisoners' wives and their struggles to preserve and affirm their families in the face of institutional and social negativity.

Chapter 2

Families and Incarceration

If you go to any prison where men are incarcerated, the visiting room is crowded with their wives, girlfriends, children, and, to a lesser extent, their mothers and other relatives. Go to a prison where women are housed, and you see few males. Mothers, sisters or friends bringing children comprise the visitors, who don't come as often or in as great numbers. Since there are fewer women incarcerated than men, there are fewer facilities. These facilities are generally located in rural areas, far from the urban centers where most families live, thus placing a burden upon the families, especially those caring for their children.

When men are in prison, women travel great distances to visit them, bring their children, send money and packages, and accept collect phone calls. Their wives and girlfriends act as a link to the outside world. When women are incarcerated, the reverse doesn't hold true. If they have an intact intimate relationship when they go in, it generally does not survive. Mothers and grandmothers may visit and bring children, but it's less frequent (E. Barry, interview, June 12, 1991). When a father is incarcerated, it is more common that the mother of his children will relocate with the children near the prison or visit with the children so that contact is maintained and the family unit is preserved (Barry, 1985a).

MALE/FEMALE SOCIALIZATION

What accounts for the difference in family support depending on whether it is the wife/mother or the husband/father who is imprisoned? As a result of the socialization process, men and women assume different roles in behavior, in how they feel about themselves, and in what they expect in life. Traditionally, women are expressive, nurturing, and selfless, while men are dominant, assertive, and instrumental. Women are expected to invest themselves in their marriages through their relationships with their husbands and children (Bem, 1974; Lester, 1982). Sheehy (1979, p. 98) states that the message for women has been "You are who you marry and who you mother." Women's experience has been "living in the rhythms of other lives," as marriage and pregnancy are what women "have always done" (Rich, 1986, pp. 25, 33).

That women from the beginning of time have taken the responsibility for feeding, teaching, and protecting the young probably led to their responsibility for feeding the entire group. Men took care of their own needs, not having the responsibility of the young, and did not care for the broader community (French, 1985). A contemporary social role interpretation views sex differences as emanating from the different social positions men and women occupy and the different role expectations that result. The overall division of labor between women and men brings about sex differences in skills, status, and power. The roles men occupy demand skills to meet defined tasks, particularly through competition, a certain emotional detachment from coworkers, and systematic decision making. The primarily domestic roles women occupy require meeting multiple goals, flexibility, and cooperation with other family members. Anticipation of needs, empathy, and emotional expressiveness are skills helpful in meeting the familial goals (Eagly, 1987).

It was deBeauvoir (1952) writing in the 1950s who directed our attention to the second-class status of women as housewives and mothers attached to the status of husbands. Yet, even with her manifesto unveiling this subordination, not much has changed—we continue to write of its existence, nearly fifty years later. The indoctrination that males and females receive occurs primarily through observation of and participation in simple, everyday patterns. These lessons are imprinted so deeply in our minds that in 1968 Broverman and others were able to test assumptions about mental health related to gender. The clinically healthy male and the clinically healthy adult were identical, contrasting with the clinically healthy female. Women were perceived as less healthy by the standards used to measure adult well-being (Broverman et al., 1972; Howe, 1979).

This socialization assumes great importance when we look at caregiving. Women's sense of self-worth and morality is embedded in social relationships. Contemporary theories of women's psychology focus on the theme of women's sense of connection and support via networks. A responsibility orientation rooted in connection and relatedness to others, as opposed to a rights orientation related to separation and autonomy, is predominant for women (Gilligan, 1982; Hancock, 1989).

Gilligan (1982, p. 17) writes: "Thus women not only define themselves in a context of social relationship but also judge themselves in terms of their ability to care. Women's place in man's life cycle has been that of nurturer, caretaker, and helpmate, the weaver of those networks of relationships on which she in turn relies." As women's sense of self becomes organized around maintaining and affirming relationships, affiliation becomes more highly valued than does self-enhancement (Miller, 1986). While the desire for affiliation is a strength,

Miller feels it also leads women into serving the needs of others, a role of subservience. Chodorow (1978) agrees that this orientation to the needs and experiences of others can result in a loss of self.

CARING BEHAVIOR

Caring is associated with women and with the places women are found—the family and the helping professions like nursing, social work, and elementary school teaching. It is taken away from men, as not caring is a defining characteristic of men (Graham, 1983). Chodorow (1978) finds men's sense of self coming from doing things for and by themselves. For example, consider this typical pattern. Wives of alcoholics often think they can alter the drinking career of their husbands through a "home treatment" (Wiseman, 1980); husbands of female alcoholics tend to leave their wives, see no reason to be involved in treatment, and often claim professional responsibilities as reasons to avoid such a commitment (Blume, 1990; Rolls, 1989).

In another example, Oliver (1983) writes that disability or ill health of a husband carries with it a universal expectation from medical staff, social services, and the husband himself that the wife will do everything necessary. Frequently her state of health and her time and abilities are not taken into consideration. Furthermore, Oliver found that wives felt that they could not in good faith abandon a sick husband, even if the marriage had been failing before the illness.

The female domestic role encourages caring behavior toward family members. Researchers have found that women provide major emotional support to their husbands and to other women—more support than they themselves receive (Belle, 1982; Bernard, 1981; Vaux, 1985). While there is no reason that social support cannot come from men, this usually is not the case. Women have more of their self-esteem and mental health connected to the success of a relationship than men do (Moffitt et al., 1986).

Men in prison are visited by their wives and mothers, whereas women in prison are visited by their mothers and sisters. Brodsky (1975) found that fathers rarely visit or write to their imprisoned sons. The role models of male support to and involvement in families that are separated do not encourage males to be relationship-oriented. Custody is granted to mothers in approximately 90 percent of divorce cases, most often agreed to by the couple or given to her by default. Furstenberg and Nord (1982) found that children tend to have little contact with the nonresidential parent. Only 16 percent of children saw their absent fathers once a week, and almost 40 percent had had no contact with their fathers in five years.

In cases of divorce, more than half of custodial mothers receive no child support. Of those who receive payments, about 30 percent receive partial payments. The data do not show that the men lack the money to pay or that the awards are too high. Rather, it seems to be connected to the fact that there is poor enforcement of the court orders (Weitzman, 1985).

Despite women's entry into the workforce, men are still not doing their share of work in the home (Hochschild, 1989; Pleck, 1979). Although men's share of housework is increasing, overwhelmingly the traditional roles of male breadwinner and female nurturer persist, continuing to validate the stereotype of the caretaking role of women (Zur-Szpiro & Longfellow, 1982).

FACTORS OF PARENTAL SEPARATION

The uniqueness of the incarcerated husband/father or wife/mother can be explained by using the "mapping sentence" for the study of parent-absent families developed by Rosenfeld and Rosenstein (1973). The mapping sentence examines eight varying factors that allow differentiation between types of parental separation and its impact on the family. It begins with X, the precipitating cause. Is the precipitating cause occupational (such as military), disability (such as mental hospital, other hospital, or prison), or is it familial disruption (such as death, divorce, or marital separation)? These categories relate primarily to the issue of stigma and to whether the absent parent will return to the family at some point. The precipitating cause also will define how the absent parent is viewed—as hero or criminal—and whether the absence is seen as a relief, unwelcome, or abandonment.

The second category includes the degrees of parental absence. This involves five factors: who is absent (mother or father); how long the absence is (short, prolonged, or permanent); frequency of absence (one time, more than one time, or recurring at regular or irregular intervals); amount of contact with absent parent (frequent, infrequent, or none); and kind of contact during absence (ranging from in-person visits and telephone calls through glass to contacts by mail or telephone).

Together these factors can develop a profile of degree of absence. The mapping sentence continues to examine the effect on the family (as a unit) and on the individual members (mother, father, children). Parent-absent families differ from families in which both parents are present. These differences can be found in examining two areas: everyday life, such as emotional hardships, economic hardship, relationships, activities, and so forth; and permanent characteristics, such as pathology, patterns of communication, and altered family structure.

Incarceration of a parent is a unique type of parental absence. We will now turn to the difference in impact on family, depending on whether that parent is the wife or the husband.

WHEN WOMEN ARE INCARCERATED

Women in prison are seen as threats to the family and the community. They have gone against the stereotypical wife/mother role, and are judged more harshly due to the threat to the family structure (Feinman, 1983). A man in prison may be "sowing his wild oats"; a woman is unladylike, rebellious. For many criminal offenses, women and men are treated equally, but for offenses considered traditionally male, such as murder and armed robbery, women receive more severe sentences than men (Jones, 1980). According to the National Coalition Against Domestic Violence, abusive men who kill their partners serve an average of two to six years; women who kill their abusive partners serve an average of 15 years. Even when women kill in self-defense, society is much harsher in its judgment.

An incarcerated woman is more frowned upon by society than an incarcerated man, and the stigma is greater for her and her family. She is not supposed to be there (interview, J. Husby, July 18, 1991). A similar situation is found when comparing female alcoholics and male alcoholics. The women are perceived more negatively, as immoral and bad (Wilson, 1980). Rolls (1989) suggests that this is because society in general perceives women more negatively than men.

A Bureau of Justice Statistics special report states that more than 76 percent of women in prison have children, whereas only 60 percent of male prisoners do. Two-thirds of these women have children under the age of 18. Prior to incarceration, nearly four out of five of the mothers had been living with their children (1991, p. 6). Most of these women are single mothers—separated, divorced, never married, widowed, or not receiving support from the father—and they are the primary source of financial and emotional support for their children (Barry, 1985a).

At the time of arrest, police officers may not necessarily ask if there are children; women may be reluctant to tell for fear of having them removed to state care. Relatives or neighbors may try to take the children in before state intervention. During the court proceedings and at the time of the jail or prison term, officials may be unaware of the children's existence or whereabouts (Stanton, 1980). Not only is the likelihood of her being the sole support of her children an issue, but separation from her children involves a greater role change as a woman and mother, striking at her personal identity and self-image (Henriques, 1982; Velimesis, 1969; Zalba, 1964). Imprisoned mothers often feel tremendous guilt and sadness that their children are placed in strange environments, perhaps separated from siblings (Fishman & Cassin, 1981).

Koban (1983) writes of key differences between prisoner mothers and prisoner fathers. Mothers who are incarcerated are more often first-time offenders, were living with their children prior to incarceration, are separated from their children for the first time, are incarcerated far from their children's home, desire to have their children visit them, have difficulty contacting their children, have infrequent contact with their children while incarcerated, have children who are separated from their siblings, plan to reunite with their children, and have strained relations with their families due to incarceration. Compared with incarcerated mothers, fathers more often are repeat offenders, were not living with their children prior to incarceration, have been separated from their children before, are incarcerated closer to home, have frequent contact with their children when visiting is desired, have children living with their other natural parent and siblings, can depend on caretakers to bring their children to visit, and think their children are happy, without problems.

The biggest impact on the family when women are incarcerated is custody of the children. The fathers are not caring for the children, and the mothers must make arrangements, if possible, with other family members. These families are primarily poor and minority. Zalba (1964) found that more African-American and Mexican-American women prisoners were able to place their children with relatives than were Caucasian women. Still, only 29 percent of all fathers were caring for their children. A 1981 study of female prisoners in North Carolina found only 14 percent of children living with their father or the father's relatives. Almost three-fourths lived with relatives of the mother (Governor's Advocacy Council on Children and Youth, 1981). While children do not automatically end up in foster families, according to Barry (1985b), more and more children are falling to the system. In California, once a child has been in foster care for 12 months, a petition can be filed for termination of parental rights based on the fact that the imprisoned parent cannot provide a home for the child. Incarcerated parents may not be adequately notified of these hearings, and then the reunification of the family upon release from prison becomes virtually impossible.

Even the way in which women and men do their time is different. On the inside, men tend to do their time alone, forming few, if any, friendships. Women tend to form substitute families among themselves, complete with kin terms (interview, S. Wing, August 10, 1991). This is a continuation of their socialization to be caretakers and connected.

There are two major contrasts between incarceration of males and females related to family interaction. First, male prisoners are more likely to have the support and visitation of female family members, whereas women are more likely to have fewer visits (especially from males), less outside contact, and less money/packages sent to them. Second, male prisoners do not tend to lose touch with their children, who are more likely to be cared for by the children's mother, whereas female prisoners, as single parents, see their children less and may lose custody of them.

WHEN MEN ARE INCARCERATED

Since the family is the basic unit of society and the location where social attachments are formed and grounded, it is interesting to note that relatively little research has been done on the value of the family in rehabilitation or on the impact of incarceration on the free family. This is all the more surprising because the few studies that have been done in relation to recidivism have been promising (Fox, 1981; Hairston, 1988a). This section examines the research on families and recidivism (which has been done only on male prisoners) and how roles change when the husband/father is incarcerated.

There has recently been an upsurge of interest in families of prisoners, in part due to the obvious failure of the "lock 'em up and throw away the key" philosophy that has not lowered crime rates, and in part due to the activism of agencies and individuals who work for prisoners' rights, constructive visiting policies, and so forth. They are forcing the agenda to change at the same time that states are realizing their departments of corrections are in fiscal crises.

REVIEW OF LITERATURE ON PRISONERS AND FAMILIES

The earliest recidivism studies pointed to positive associations between family ties and post-release success. These include a study by Ohlin (1954) of men released between 1925 and 1935, in which he found that 75 percent of the prisoners who had maintained "active family interest" while in prison were successful, compared with 34 percent of those classified as "loners." Glaser (1964) used Ohlin's classifications, with similar results, with federal prisoners. An earlier Glaser study of prisoners who where released in 1940–49 in Illinois revealed a 74 percent success rate for prisoners with active family contact, compared with a 43 percent success rate for prisoners who were loners.

More recent recidivism studies were carried out in the 1970s to early 1980s. The study most often cited is that done by Holt and Miller (1972) for the California Department of Corrections. This one-year study followed 412 men who had been paroled from the Southern Conservation Center, and produced findings quite similar to the Ohlin and Glaser works. Examination of the number of different visitors prisoners had in their last year of incarceration, revealed that 70 percent of those with three visitors were arrest-free in their first year of parole. This compared with a success rate of 50 percent for the loners.

Adams and Fischer (1976) followed 124 men paroled from the Hawaii State Prison in 1969 and 1970. Comparing the number of letters and visits from family and friends, they found that 9 out of 12 observations confirmed their hypothesis that nonrecidivists had more outside contact than the recidivists.

Massachusetts prisoners were studied by LeClair (1978), who followed 878 prisoners released in 1973 and 841 released in 1974. Recidivism rates were examined, comparing those who participated in the home furlough program with those who did not. In both years, the recidivism rates were lower for those who participated in the furlough program.

Burstein (1977) compared prisoners who had regular visits with prisoners who had conjugal visits. Although the men with conjugal visits had a lower recidivism rate, it was not statistically significant. However, this is the only study not revealing a significant difference, and this might be accounted for by the fact that he did not compare his groups with prisoners receiving no visitors, as other studies had done.

A 1982 study by Howser and MacDonald of 540 prisoners in New York's prisoner conjugal visiting program showed a recidivism rate of 67 percent less than expected, compared with the overall return rate of New York parolees.

IMPORTANCE OF FAMILY ROLES

Hughes (1945) distinguishes between master and auxiliary status traits. A master trait functions to distinguish those who belong from those who don't. Race functions as such a trait, so that a nonwhite doctor or other upper-status occupation would seem out of place based on auxiliary traits that should apply to the status of minority individual. Becker (1963, pp. 33–34) states that criminal, or deviant, also acts as a master status because it is achieved through rule-breaking. The individual is identified first as a deviant ("What kind of person would break a rule?"), and then other identifications can be made. There is a common assumption that prisoners cannot be good husbands or fathers, for example, because of their stigmatized master status.

What is it about family relationships that would have such an impact on the rehabilitation of these prisoners? Carrying out family roles allows an individual to be connected to society; the lack of roles contributes to normlessness. Yet marital and parental roles are altered when a man goes to prison. Wives who attempt to involve their husbands in the family despite the obvious hardships allow for the continuation of their social roles.

In her study of 30 prisoners' wives, Fishman (1990) found that the women worked hard at preserving the image that their husbands were important members of the household. Regardless of the criminal behavior and negative impact of the separation, the women treated the men as significant in disciplining the children, in decision-making, and in providing emotional support. These women rarely labeled their husbands as deviant, rationalizing that they had "made a mistake." In their total orientation to their husbands through visits, letters, phones calls, and plans, they almost desperately ignored the lopsided nature of the relationship. Resources flowed to the men, without the normal give-and-take of a relationship.

What made waiting for their husbands especially difficult was "the suspension of their identities. They were their husbands' wives, and had no other significant roles to play" (Fishman, 1990, p. 195). This phenomenon of wives attached to their husbands' status is seen also in other relationships where, while the husband is not in a stigmatized position, he is frequently absent . The marriage helps the husband in his role, but the wife does not receive reciprocal benefits. This often holds for ministers' wives who are expected to focus on the husbands' career (Wells, 1974); college football players' wives, who are frequently left alone and have worries about injuries and losing (Mosher, 1954); and corporate wives, who are expected by the company to provide a sanctuary at home so the husbands can focus all their energies on the frenetic pace and demands of corporate work. Furthermore, like prisoners' wives, corporate wives are expected to move frequently, a factor that disrupts their lives (Lake, 1973; Seidenberg, 1974; Whyte, 1951).

Social relationships are based on reciprocity, but prisoners are very limited in what they can do for their families. Prisons deprive their wards of mobility, possessions, money (to any great extent), resources, and individuality. Rarely do prisoners earn enough money to send home. More commonly, the family sends money to the prisoner's account. Prisoners may not have access to simple items like birthday cards. Even the phone call home is a collect call. His removal from the mainstream deprives the prisoner of the opportunity to sustain and create social relationships (Holt & Miller, 1972).

The women in Koenig's study (1985) similarly tried to continue the myth that the man was the head of the household. They held traditional views of the wife's roles as supporter and nurturer, and the husband's roles in marriage and family life as those of decision-maker, wage earner, and disciplinarian. Since the husband cannot continue these roles, the wife increases her supporter and nurturer role, and the husband becomes increasingly dependent upon her. In fact, as the wife begins to take over more of the roles the husband formally carried out, she may turn to him for emotional support. This may be difficult for him to provide, and his dependent role increases.

Koenig (1985) states that the alterations in roles change the nature of visits. Many of these women, rather than discuss life on the outside, focus on life when the husband will be released, the "fantasy life." This fantasy life revolves around a happier time in the future. Joan Husby, director of Friends Outside in Salinas, California, stated in an interview (July 18, 1991) that the combination of separation and reunion itself creates a bond for many couples. Their lives revolve around the lack of time together and the distance between them, with planning for the future a priority in their lives. It is very difficult for many couples to be present-oriented. The future planning gives them something to focus on.

Prisoners themselves attempt to maintain their former roles as husbands and fathers. In letters and during visits they may counsel their children about schoolwork, and try to influence their behavior in the community (Swan, 1981). In the prison setting, however, the men are not encouraged to fulfill their parental obligations, and there is little support given to them in that regard (Hairston, 1988b). For example, children are not allowed to bring their homework into the visiting rooms of most prisons, where fathers could interact with them in an appropriate role behavior.

The most common hardships reported by wives of prisoners include loneliness, financial problems, disciplining children, adjusting to role changes, and concern for their husbands' safety and well-being. These areas are the same as those cited by military wives (Boynton & Pearce, 1978; McCubbin & Dahl, 1976; Rienerth, 1978). These "waiting wives" are affected by the instability of separation, aloneness, and role ambiguity. Role ambiguity is particularly difficult for two reasons. While prisoners' wives and military wives are supposed to support their husbands in maintaining the family, in the case of the former, and in encouraging the military career, in the case of the latter, there are many messages of the women's movement that say this assistance should not be at the expense of the well-being and happiness of the woman. Yet providing this support does create hardship. Furthermore, there are no role models for married, but alone, women in our society. The women do not know how to act toward others, and others are unsure how to act toward them (Boynton & Pearce, 1978).

It is the wife's role that will undergo the greatest change during separation. In a situation like that of the wives of prisoners of war, wives become increasingly independent as the family becomes more female-centered. These families do not know whether the husband will return, nor does the military community know how to deal with them—are they still part of the military community or not? The stresses of prolonged separation under these conditions create an adaptation that lessens the possibility of successful reunion (Rienerth, 1978).

In fact, Holt and Miller (1972) point out that some prisoners' wives develop the "service wife syndrome"—like some military wives, they adapt to separation and get along better when there is absence. When the soldier-husband returns, roles in the family have altered so much that the husband has no role to play in the household. His going back to duty becomes a relief to both of them.

Unfortunately, prisons do not keep statistics on how many divorces of prisoners occur in any given year. Burstein (1977) reports that during their first few years of incarceration the divorce rate among prisoners is significantly higher than that of the general population. Holt and Miller (1972) found that many wives divorced their husbands in the second year of incarceration, but that there was a strong core of women who stayed married for the long term, even through repeated incarcerations.

In the chapters that follow, we shall examine the specific impacts of incarceration on the wives of prisoners. Women's other-orientation plays a role in the wife's devotion to her husband, in spite of the hardship it imposes on her. Using the words of prisoners' wives and findings from similar studies, we will explore the experience of the caretaker when family life is played out in the prison setting.

Part II
DATA

Chapter 3

Living with Secrets

I feel kind of bad. Sometimes I envy couples. I do that a lot, see couples walking down the street.   Then I'll see some married couples, young people, having everything that they want. And I think about how, wow, look at me, I'm doing it all by myself. My husband is incarcerated. It's very stressful. And then not telling people, it really bothers me. Sometimes when people ask, "Oh, are you married?" . . . I get a funny vibe. (Sharon)

I wanted to see really what people thought. So they knew what was going on. "You're just going to have to live with it. You've got to make your own bed, so you lie in it." That type of thing. And then I said, "We broke up." And I've never seen so many happy people in the world. And to this day there's people who think we broke up. It was just a lot easier. I'm rid of them. My best, best friends, of course, know. But there's several people, "Oh, thank God, she left him. Now she can have a decent life." (Pat)

My dad liked J___ a lot until he found out he'd been in prison. And then instead of taking J___ on his own merits and knowing the kind of person he was from meeting J___, he more or less said, "Well, he had been in prison in L___," and when he went back in they didn't take into consideration what he had been like since the robbery. And they just decided, "Oh, well, he's not good enough for my daughter." And I said, "Well, I think he is." And he decided I wasn't good enough to be a daughter. (Cyndi)

A major cause of anxiety and concern for the wife of a prisoner is whether to tell others about her husband's incarceration. This decision will color how she relates to her family, friends, coworkers, and employers. Rollo (1988) sums up wives' experience: Because she supports her husband, her family may reject her, she may need to move, or she may be fired from her job. There may be pressure from some friends to break up, while others are intolerant and refuse to discuss it. Other friends just don't know what to say. This experience somewhat parallels response after a divorce, according to Goode (1956). Kinship or friendship doesn't guarantee support in time of divorce. A decision will be made as to whether the family or friends support the breakup of the family, approve of the conduct of the divorcee, or are friendly to the other spouse.

Another consideration, according to Holt and Miller (1972), is that keeping incarceration a secret restricts the number of contacts the prisoner has with the outside. Regardless of what the wife is facing, the new prisoner generally wants to maintain social contacts if at all possible. Stigma experienced by the prisoner is usually related to the crime committed—for example, whether he is a child molester or a check forger. Ostracism is also influenced by the cumulative effect of repeated offenses. If the couple decides not to tell family and friends, the social world of the prisoner is limited.

STIGMA

The wife needs to decide if she will speak openly and freely, or with omission and half-truths. The element of creating and maintaining a secretive or partly secretive life requires consistency. She must be on her guard not to be discovered, thus creating a pressure most wives do not encounter. The reason for this secrecy rests in the wife's perception that the stigma of her prisoner husband's status will harm her job or housing prospects and her personal relationships.

As Goffman discusses in *Stigma* (1963), once a prisoner has been labeled, his family is affected by the loss of status in the community and by societal hostility. The family suffers from a "courtesy stigma" because they are affiliated with the stigmatized. The courtesy stigma is attached through the formal means of trial, criminal labeling, and incarceration, and through the informal mechanisms of hostility and lessened respect toward the family, which they internalize as shame.

The wife perceives this threat from observation of the collective societal reaction to prisoners, as well as from the experiences she hears from other prisoners' wives. Fishman (1990) reports that while wives in her study experienced feelings of shame because of society's stigmatization of prisoners, these feelings were secondary to the acute feelings of loneliness due to separation from their husbands and the pressing demands of everyday life—child care, work, legal matters. Still, they did feel discredited and devalued due to their husbands' offenses.

Morris (1965) found that wives feared gossip about their husbands' imprisonment more than they actually experienced hostility. They were ashamed of what people might say about both the incarceration and the loss of a man from their household. Generally they were not ashamed of what their husbands had done.

Families of prisoners tend to rationalize the crimes by saying their loved ones had "made a mistake, and everyone makes a mistake at some time in their life.

People should be forgiven for mistakes and given another chance." Reframing the experience to focus on their spouse rather than the victim is a coping mechanism. Aside from mentioning the mistake perspective, only one wife mentioned in an interview anything about the impact of her husband's crime. In that instance, the wife referred to the "dirty" drug money her husband brought home. One time she ripped up the money and told him not to bring this money into the home. But then she thought better of it—she needed the money, and the drug dealing continued without her further comment.

Many wives in this study were married to men who were convicted of violent crimes. Yet they, too, believed the men were still valuable human beings worthy of their care and attention. For example, one wife whose husband committed murder said she married him because she "really liked his values." A girlfriend whose partner killed a man while drunk explained it away by referring to the drinking and the fact that he was a nonviolent man who had never been in any trouble before. While I did not question the women specifically about how they felt about the victims of their husbands' crimes, the injustice these women focused on clearly related to the difficulty of their own present situation.

REACTION OF FAMILY AND FRIENDS

We live in a society with a couple orientation, where every individual is expected to date, to marry, and to have a family including children. Parents dream of this for their children, children are socialized to want this, adolescents fear and desire it, and young adults long for it. Our coupling will make us complete. Women will have the status of "wife" and "mother," be acknowledged as adults, and have a place in the social order. Yet, as Steese (1988) points out, prisoners' wives exist in a state of personal social limbo—neither really married, single, widowed, nor divorced.

Not all marriages, however, are equally valued. For the wife or fiancée of a prisoner, the cherished coupling is thrust into doubt, distaste, or ambivalence. It is often discredited; it is rarely joyous. The idealized picture-book relationship, which exists nowhere in reality, is applied even more vigorously to the prisoner and his wife. The mass media images of the prisoner as a sadistic, asocial, brutal, and calculating man eliminates all possibility that he could be considerate, gentle, giving, and loving. There is always a lingering doubt about rehabilitation. Family, friends and the public at large see little gray, and focus on black or white. Tricia Hedin writes (1986, p. 14), "Few marriages come under such close scrutiny as those of inmates and their spouses. . . . There are pitying smiles, silent reproaches, numerous questions and shocked responses." And Koenig (1985, p. 44) writes, "Reaction to the man's offense may include shock, disgust, curiosity, pity, and fear. . . . People may wonder why a woman would stay with or choose such a man."

When B___ was arrested, I was in the Bay Area visiting with my family. When I got the call, I left immediately. Everybody was shocked because it is totally out of

B___'s character. Right on through the conviction, no one could believe it. . . . My family held back their feelings on it, their reactions, until the conviction. They don't have too much to say about B___ anymore. They feel that if a jury of 12 people found him guilty, then he's guilty. There's no question in their mind. (Carrie)

When I was first with him, I was sharing a house with a girlfriend and she was shocked. I couldn't even get letters from him at the house because she didn't want him to know her address. And I finally had to move to pursue my relationship with him. So that's when I moved [into my sister-in-law's house]. And I severed ties with her altogether. We'd been close friends for a lot of years, but she couldn't handle it. (Marilyn)

Most of the 20 women in Koenig's 1985 study received no support from their parents or adult children. They found more help from friends or, in some cases, from the church. Politically motivated hysteria about crime and criminals numbs our ability to reach out to the less fortunate. Our fear overwhelms our humane tendencies toward help, rehabilitation, and forgiveness. The deprived individual (whether deprived of love, a home, education, respect, money, mental ability, etc.) who commits a criminal act becomes, in our minds, depraved. The prisoner is seen as a permanent loser, with no redeeming qualities.

My cousin's brother-in-law said, "You don't need to mess around with that, you can find something better." (Janet)

The only social negative stigma I get from J___ being in prison is from long-time associates and some nonassociates who feel that my waiting for someone with that much time [is a waste]. But what they don't realize is that that someone is my husband and was my husband before he went, because I made a vow to him stating "until death do us part," and not if or in case he goes to prison and gets a lot of time. Also, not only did I make this vow to my husband and myself when we say "I do," we're making it to the originator of the marriage arrangement, Jehovah God. (Charlene)

[I received negative reaction] from a lot of his daughter's friends. "He committed murder, he's where he belongs. You should forget about him and go on with your life." That type of thing. (Betty)

Family support and acceptance may be gradual, or split between members of the family. The wife may be pulled between her family and her in-laws. Her parents may urge her to "leave the bum," while his parents may blame her for his behavior (Schwartz & Weintraub, 1974). The wife makes choices as to what's best for her couple unity. In all cases, she needs a strength and commitment to the marriage beyond what couples ordinarily need because she is fighting the doubts and hostility of her and/or his family, on top of the degradations and problems of the prison system. She must believe that she can make it despite the odds.

My mom, she don't say much. And my sister, "I wouldn't marry no jailbird." But I said, "I love him and I care for him." So they were all against him. That's why I moved out here. Because they weren't supporting me at all. I just moved away from them. I'll go on my own, I got that attitude. "I don't need you, anyway. You're not supporting my man. If you're going to try to support me without my man, I can't deal with it." (Minerva)

They were very cold. They still don't like the fact. I'd say that my family is not prejudiced in any way as far as that goes [she is white; he is black], but the fact that he's in prison is a kind of prejudice. And I've had to tell them that it's my life. "I'm not affecting you in any way and I don't expect you to affect me." And my mom, she's come around. I think that actually by the time that he gets out, maybe that we both will be accepted wholeheartedly. It's going to take awhile. (Terri)

I didn't even tell my family about R___ until after R___ and I were married for six months. My mother came to visit me last year, and while we were standing at the airport taking her luggage off the wheel as it's going around, she knew I was visiting a man in prison, and she said, "Are you still seeing that guy in prison?" And I said, "Your son-in-law? If we're going to fight about this, you're going to give me a hard time, we can leave your luggage on here. I've made my decision." (Misty)

Schneller (1976) found in his study of 93 couples that few friends were lost over the incarceration. If friends were likely to object to the imprisonment, they were given other excuses for the absence (e.g., he was in the army or working in another city). However, most families belonged to a subculture where incarceration was a part of life and not a reason to cut off a friendship. In the present study, family reaction is influenced in some cases by the fact that another family member, a brother or father, had previously been incarcerated.

See, the reason why I don't stay with my mother is because of my husband. Me and her have a lot of problems. Like my mother sees me going through the same things she went through. But my father was not really in jail as much as my husband is now. He was into drugs and the same things. And my mother, she don't really knock him for doing what he's doing and why he's in jail and everything, but my mother, she don't think about how it was, how she wouldn't let my father go, and how much she wanted to wait on him. When my father was going back and forth to jail, my mother was right there. She just [tells me], "I did it. I'm telling you about it, and I know, I experienced it, so just take my advice. Don't do it. Leave him alone. Leave him there. You don't want to go through that." Me and her don't get along with that because I don't like to hear that. (Tijuan)

In the beginning, no one knew I was going to marry him. I made some little remarks to my mother, but she figured I was kidding. And then, she did say a few things like, "Well, what are you going to do with him? He doesn't have a job, he can't do anything for you." . . . She won't knock him down because of his mistake. In fact, my brother just got out of prison. He was in Soledad, too. So I guess she kinda figured that she was in the same situation as another mother would be, a child being incarcerated. So, she's kinda encouraging me now. (Sharon)

[My mother and stepfather] have both spent time in prison. They were writing bogus checks and got caught. Basically I wasn't around it too much then because I was busy with my own life. Had he made a deal, she wouldn't have served time in prison. T___ made a deal to keep me out. I can say, "Well, at least T___ kept me out of jail. What did E___ do for you?" She spent three years, he spent five. (Valerie)

While a wife may be alienated from her family, often there are some family members who do support her, who come around gradually, or members of her husband's family who give her encouragement, material assistance, rides to the prison, and so forth. In these cases, taking the risk of openness about the marriage has paid off. These family members help to balance the instances where other members have rejected the marriage or cannot be told about the marriage. Daniel and Barrett (1981) report that while in one study 88 percent of wives could name at least one family member who was usually helpful, on average the wife's family and the in-law family could at best be described as only "sometimes helpful."

His family, they're supportive. He has all brothers, and they've been through this with him before, as far as him doing time. So they feel like, well, he got his wife now, that's what he need most of all, his wife. So they're supportive of me for sure. I can always go to them if I need anything, a ride down there or something like that. . . . He feels like he should get a lot more visits from them. His mother visits him all the time. . . . He call them all the time. They talk to him, keep in contact that way. As far as going down and visit, they give all the time to me. I'm more than happy. (Wanda)

My mom and dad said, "That's it. Sue, you've been through enough. No more. I mean, you are crazy if you stick with him." So I had a lot of opposition. In fact, more opposition than support. But my brother and his wife, they said, "Sue, we know that R___'s a beautiful person, don't give up on him now." Now everybody sees that I'm totally dedicated and that R___ and I are making this marriage work. And they're seeing such a neat change in R___ that they all love him. My mom and dad love him. Everybody loves R___ now. And so they've really forgiven him, they're really sticking by him. They're totally supporting him through the lawyers, through everything. So now I've got the support group, the whole family. (Sue)

I think R___ totally impressed [my mother]. She thought he was going to be a guy in there with an eighth-grade education, and it really shocked her. So my mother is supportive of me now. The rest of the family patronizes me. [My two brothers] chose that if I happen to go to Florida to visit, to leave him here, even if he gets paroled. But that's fine. I don't choose to go to Florida to visit. . . . I don't feel that I'm losing my family because I married R___. I feel like my family is losing out on a really super person. (Misty)

I do have main support from my mother, who has helped me tremendously in times of distress, financially, mentally, and emotionally. I also have a big Christian family who have encouraged me spiritually not to let anything separate me from the love of God and Christ. I do have friends I can talk to. I only talk to mature friends about my personal situation. I also have Elders in the congregation that I can go to and have went to when I've needed encouragement to keep going spiritually, since this spiritual aspect of me has kept me sane in dealing with this situation mentally. J___ is an only child and doesn't have any relatives in California except one who is pretty up in age, [and] to put it in small words, he disowned J___ when he went to prison. (Charlene)

Extended family assistance does differ by racial group. Hairston (1988a) points out that black family literature indicates strong subcultural expectations of family aid among black families. Research by Hays and Mindel (1973) concluded that the extended kin network of black families is more salient than it is for white families. In general, the social support literature, as reviewed by Vaux (1985), points to black and Hispanic families turning more to family and friends than to external sources of support. This becomes significant when the ethnic composition of prisoners is examined. Prisoners are disproportionately minorities. At the time of this study (1986), California prisoners were 65 percent nonwhite. The support from extended families becomes a more urgent need when the husband is in prison.

On balance, most reaction from family and friends is mixed. Parents and siblings have many reservations and are hesitant to support the marriage. The family members may not be a unified front, especially when considering the wife's family and the prisoner's family together. Some are supportive to varying degrees, others may sever ties. Friends may not know how to be supportive because they perceive the relationship as a limitation, not as a source of joy. The wife is lonely, dealing with unusual problems. The hesitation or outright lack of support does not deter the wives. Their commitment to the marriage outweighs their ties to family and friends. However, given the nature of the difficulty of maintaining a prison marriage, this support is sorely needed. It is exactly what the wife needs, yet she usually will have to carry on without it. Brown et al. (1975) found that when women faced difficult life challenges, having a supportive confidant was an effective buffer against depression. It is other prisoners' wives who become her primary support, not necessarily kin or friends.

[My daughter] is cautiously optimistic. She would like to be happy about it, but she's afraid to be. But she will not interfere either. My mother does not understand this. My mother will not even attempt to understand it. She will not accept it, not at this point, and I don't think she ever will. I talk to her about it, but she will not listen. . . . Maybe with time, maybe not. It will not change things between R___ and I if she doesn't. (Isabel)

My stepmother, my father, my sister-in-law, they visit me or I go visit them. But now my father's filled out forms to come visit B___. But my mother and stepfather just kind of back off from the whole situation. So I figure that's their prerogative. (Carrie)

His sister is pretty supportive. But her attitude is, "I love you because you are Marie, not because you're married to my brother, not because you go visit my brother." Whenever I go there, she's always, "Why don't you spend the day with me today and go tonight? Let's go to the beach." Her attitude is more or less, we have our lives to live. "I'm sorry that P___ got in this situation, and it's too bad that he got into the situation, but it's no sense putting us in it, too, because of it." And that's really nice to have her attitude like that. Whereas his mother, when it comes time for family visits, she wants me to sit by the phone and wait for the phone to ring. My attitude is, if I'm home, I'll get the call, and if I'm not, they'll call me next weekend. I can't sit there and wait for the phone to ring. And her attitude is that I should get off work early to be home to get his telephone calls, I should leave work early to make it down there by the six o'clock bus. (Marie)

The decision as to whether to tell others outside family is a difficult one. Some prisoners' wives don't tell anyone and let people assume they are single women. Some tell close friends. Others tell people at work who will need to know in case of needed time off for family visiting. Some let it be known without broadcasting it. But the decision to tell is related to the stigma others in society attach to criminals, the "guilt by association" reaction that prisoners' wives expect and dread. Many dislike the questioning that may follow. So they balance the desire to share about their marriage with the anticipated negative reaction that their marriage is to a prisoner. Like women who are single due to widowhood or divorce, of whom only a minority continue to have a social network from their married lives (Weiss, 1979), the friendships of a prisoner's wife also narrow.

I remember [my friends and I] went out one night, and this was before I asked W___ to marry me, and I said, "I want to marry him." And [one friend] says, "What do we call you now, Bonnie and Clyde?" They have a good sense of humor. And I said, "Well, I guess you can if you want to." (JoAnna)

It depends on who I come in contact with whether or not I reveal my situation. It also depends on my frame of mind when I come in contact with people. One thing for sure, I'm not afraid or ashamed of my situation, because everyone's entitled to one mistake in life and it can happen to anyone. But it's definitely not a secret to those who know I'm married. (Charlene)

I know a lot of people who avoid telling. Some of the women with . . . kids avoid telling the school or avoid employers. But I'm not a good liar, never have been, so I don't do it. I can't omit things, 'cause you get caught in it. My daughters' teachers know their father is an inmate. That way when situations arise that it does affect their schoolwork, they are aware of it and they are aware of why. It makes it much easier. When we have family visiting, they have to miss school, I don't have to lie to explain that. I don't have to explain it away and my kids are aware that I'm lying. I don't lie to my kids and they don't lie to me. In some instances, I guess it makes life more difficult, and some people will look at us differently. But I am so up-front that most people can't look too far down on me. Think what you want, but it's not going to affect me. It's not going to change how I feel. Accept me for what I am, or don't accept me. That's the way I've always felt it had to be. (Carrie)

The only friends I can really deal with is maybe the ones who are in the same situation I'm in. Then I talked to this lady the other day at work and she was telling me, "Well, it's not a bad thing or anything." Maybe I can help him. But I don't really talk to her because a lot of people want to know your business and things like that. Like now, some people at work know I'm married, some don't. Some ask me, I tell them, "Yeah," some I tell them, "No." So I've kinda got them confused at work because they sit up and talk about you and things like that. Like one of the ladies I work with, she said the same thing, "Why would she want a husband in jail?" That's the first thing a person would ask, "Why? Why would she want a husband in jail?" Sometimes I'm embarrassed. (Sharon)

My circle of friends has shrunk. I found out who the friends really were and who were just acquaintances. There are three friends, the rest were all acquaintances. . . . I don't get invited to places I used to go. I am getting invited to do things that people would not have invited me to do before. All of a sudden they think if I could fall in love with an inmate, that I could do a lot of other things, too. My morals are now being questioned where they never were before. (Isabel)

TELLING EMPLOYERS

Most prisoners' wives know someone who has lost a job, or have themselves lost jobs, because of their intimate association with a prisoner. The need for an income then outweighs the desire to be honest about their lives. Usually the wives need to tell a coworker or their boss in order to get time off for family visits, but otherwise, the risk may not be worth it. Most of the women interviewed by Koenig (1985) reported at least two situations in which they had been harassed or discriminated against, usually by landlords, prospective employers, and/or neighbors. And wives in Schneller's study (1976) expressed embarrassment at telling their bosses where their husbands were.

I made the mistake of telling the fast food place, and that translated into me losing that job. 'Cause my work habits never changed, I was there every day on time, I still did all the work. I was working on the cash register, I never came up short, and I had just started training to go on as a career assistant manager. And it was at that time that I told the manager, and there was something different after that. [The manager] asked quite a few questions, why he was in there, and questions like that. It was not really what's happened since then. A lot of people, they don't comprehend, okay, this happened then, but somebody can change. [I told] because even though my husband's in prison, I'm generally an honest person, which isn't so good at times, and she was going to be giving me more hours and I was going to be taking more responsibility. . . . I figure, he did the crime, he's doing the time, that should be enough. I since have learned to kind of keep to myself. I've thought things like that because it's more likely that they look at me as who did the crime. (Cyndi)

My job, I don't tell them. My boss, she knows. She's very understanding. That's the only way I can keep my job, because when family visits come up, I mean, why lie?

What's in the dark soon comes to light. And he's not, it ain't like he's getting out tomorrow, to tell a little white lie and get away with it. But he's in there for a while, and she's been very understanding. And I told her, "My husband is in jail and I have family visits, and I would like to go on the days when they call me for standby." And she asked, "What is he in for?" I told her tickets. It was really none of her business. But I just said he was in for tickets, parole violations, he wasn't supposed to drive. Sometimes it pays off to tell a lie. I mean, if I had said he's in there for selling drugs, she could've found a joint on the floor somewhere and she'd say, "Well, Tijuan's husband's in jail for selling drugs, so she smokes it." That's why it's cool to keep your private life out of it sometimes. That's really none of her business. (Tijuan)

I'm not very open. For a long time I was using the fact that he was in the army. You know, once I tell them that he's at some base, they be quiet about it. But, like my personal friends, my boss, my ex-bosses down the line, they all knew and they were all very cooperative in the fact that if I had to leave for a family visit, I had to leave. I was very fortunate. . . . It's really funny because all of them either had someone who was in there or have been in there, and so they were really good. I will always tell a job up front because of the fact of visiting and family visiting. If they want me bad enough to do the job they want me to do, they'll accept it. If they don't, they won't. But I feel it's better to be honest than to have them find out down the line somewhere. (Terri)

TELLING CHILDREN

Some parents choose not to tell their children the truth about the father's prison term, saying he is at school, in the army, working in another city, or in the hospital (Morris, 1967; Schwartz and Weintraub, 1974). This often is related to the degree of involvement the children have in terms of whether they witnessed the arrest and were present at the trial (Lowenstein, 1986).

Lowenstein (1986) found that younger children were constantly misled about the imprisonment. Parents may do this in the belief that the children are too young to understand, that the children will feel negatively toward the father if told the truth, or to protect the children from the teasing of other children. The story may be maintained even if the children visit at the prison, the parents not realizing that children can often sense the truth regardless of what they have been told (Fishman & Cassin, 1981). In fact, deception can exacerbate the children's difficulty in coping, adding to school and behavioral problems (Friedman & Esselstyn, 1965; Rosenfeld & Rosenstein, 1973).

The children of prisoners also have to deal with the stigma attached to their fathers' incarceration. They visit their dads and go on family visits. Being at the prison becomes the only time of family unity the children experience. The frequency of visits, travel time, and arrangements become a significant factor in their lives. They may miss out on activities with other children. Other children may tease them about not having their father at home. If they know about their dads being in prison, they may be taunted. The children will also be affected by how open their mothers are about the incarceration (Morris, 1967).

Most of [their friends] do know where R___ is at. I've taught them not to be ashamed of it. I told them they were going to face some ridicule when people did find out. They all want their names changed. They're still using my maiden name, and they all want his last name. And we discussed that. . . . We had great talks on whether they should tell their friends at school, and I believed in being honest. I have nothing to hide. I'm not ashamed of R___. I'm not ashamed that he's an inmate. And I think that's rubbed off on them, 'cause they're not, either. . . . I think mainly they didn't have any problems because they were so honest about it. I think if we had tried to cover it up, then an officer would have said something to his kid, "Well, his mother visits the prison." It would have been harder for them. But I think the honesty has kept them from having problems. (Misty)

I believe some of [their friends] do know. Because they feel proud of him. "I'm going to go see my dad." It doesn't bother them, and I don't think they've been teased. Here in Soledad, especially, because a lot of kids have their parents in jail. My daughters go through other harassments because they're half black. (Minerva)

A SECRET LIFE

Not sharing the truth about being married and the lifestyle concerns of being a prisoner's wife mean, in effect, that these women lead a secret life. One impact of this is that they are denied outlets for grieving about the separation (Fishman & Cassin, 1981). The truth is selective—different family members, friends, and coworkers know different aspects of their lives, ranging from all of the truth to none of the truth. Interactions within a single day vary, depending on what level of truth is known to the other person. Fishman (1990, p. 126) claims that impression management occupied the women in her study to a considerable extent. The women would ask themselves, "How can I project an image of normalcy to others despite my husband's criminal status?"

Living a secret life is not desirable to any of these women. It's painful and confusing. It doesn't feel right, but it does feel necessary. According to Koenig (1985), the wife's ability to live a stable and happy life in the community will be connected to her ability to balance her prison-oriented life and her life on the outside.

I hate it. I hate it. That's why I can't wait till he gets out here, and when he's with me, it will be different because I [won't] care. I'll have everything I want, right there, and I could give a damn about what anybody thinks. But right now I have enough things to think about and enough mental situations to go through without having to deal with everybody tripping on me. I just don't feel I even wanna deal with it, and I don't. It's hard within yourself to have to [live a secret life] 'cause you have to be on your toes all the time, constantly making up all these things and remembering everything. It's hard, I don't like it. I hate it. I don't wanna have to do that. [On my last family visit] I said that I was in Nebraska. So I even had to talk to everybody that's been there and call up there to find out about the weather. You wouldn't believe the things I went through to prove that I was really in Nebraska! Checking out the flight transactions, what airlines I went on, and you name it. (Cynthia)

I don't like that at all, it really bothers me. But it's easier than having to explain, because immediately when you say he's in prison, people say, "What did he do?" "It's none of your business." "What do you mean, what kind of man is he?" Then they go on and on, and you're just like, "I don't want to talk about it." Even my best friend, who understands me and the situation, can't accept the fact. It's hard for her to deal with. (Marie)

I don't really like [having a secret life] because I'm very, very honest with people in the sense of I really like to let people know who I am and where I'm coming from. I don't like to hide anything. But I feel like I'm always hiding something. Like up at [my son's] school, I can say to different people, and there's only a few people that I've really felt led to share it with, just because I've sensed something. They weren't judgmental or whatever, and I've sensed I can open up to them. . . . There's always the kind of cringe inside of me when they ask, "Where is your husband?" And I have to, in a sense, lie. That's what I feel. I usually say he's working, he's a mover and that he's gone out of town. So I lie, I have to lie. I just keep it to that. He's home, and we're together, you know, everyone thinks we have a happy little home here. (Sue)

Chapter 4

Relationship Realities

At first I wasn't going to marry him, 'cause at first the understanding was we'd see where the relationship went. But it was so restrictive at Folsom, I thought if I ever wanted to get to know him and try to work out a marriage—and I already decided that I liked his ideas. And I really love my husband, I love the person that he is—not the gangster in him, but his soul, his attitude toward family. I think we entered our marriage with some real positive ideas. So we got married because it was the best way for us to pursue our relationship. (Marilyn)

Yes, the loneliness is bad. Sometimes it gets very depressing, especially, like I say, when you don't have the friends around anymore. The sexual desire, I have always been a sexually active person, but the sexual desire—and I say it's the Lord—He took it away. He took it away when I'm not with my husband. The only thing that bothers me, I go dancing, which he agrees to, the only thing I don't do is dance slow, and I don't go home with anybody or anything like that. I see other couples together, and that really brings me down. In fact, I've stopped going dancing now for a while because of that, and then they play our old songs that we love, and that really gets me down. So I decided it's just better to stay away from it. (Terri)

I dream that me and him have a nice house or apartment, we have our own car. Then eventually we have a little girl, last child, and we share a lot of things together. And I want to take him to church. I want to do a lot of family activities. Be together. And I never really experienced him with my son. I have dreams about them playing outside, football and stuff like that. I always dream like that, especially when I'm listening to music. [He talks about the future] all the time. "I can just see me and my son, we're going to go here, go there. We're going to leave you at home." I say, "Go right ahead." (Tijuan)

Stress of separation, lack of privacy, lack of adequate communication and support, social stigma, financial hardship, children without their father's presence, loneliness, and prison system rules and degradation take an enormous toll on these relationships. What changes will the relationships undergo? If married before the sentencing, the wives' identities abruptly shift to that of prisoners' wives. They lose their husbands as active partners in their households, and their roles as husbands and wives change (Fishman, 1990). Rollo and Adams (1987) point out that wives feel intense grief, as with any loss, when their husbands are incarcerated. Shock is the first response, usually followed by anger and depression. Will the couple become closer, or will this experience pull them apart? How will the family unit survive?

INCARCERATION AS POSITIVE

In many cases, the women believe incarceration is a positive experience for the men. Now that they have been sentenced and forced to undergo this trauma, maybe they will change their ways and reform. Being in prison may force the prisoner to examine his actions and life direction (Rollo & Adams, 1987). Irwin (1980) writes that a short period of imprisonment can be a "respite" for felons who were caught up in self-destructive lifestyles, and hence a positive time to pull themselves together. Sharing their problems also may mature the couple and bring them closer together.

It sounds real strange, but it's kind of like his going to prison is better for our relationship. We learned a lot of things. We both grew up quite a bit. Everybody told me not to get married to him because I should be more on my own and see what it's like in there before I got married. Now I'm doing that, I'm living on my own more or less, but I still have somebody special to share it with. I don't like him being in prison, but it's helped bring us closer together, having to share the different problems, the unusual problems that come with having to be in prison. (Cyndi)

He's a much better person, I can see it. I've got a picture of him when he was on the street. He looked like he'd been run through the mill. Whereas the pictures now, I tell myself this doesn't even look like him, it looks like somebody else. It's a total 360 degrees turnaround. "If this is what it took for you to be straightened out, then I guess this is the way it's supposed to be," I told him, "You could be six feet under and dead, you could be crippled for life, but this is the way the Lord wanted you to see that what you're doing wasn't right. And this is His way of settling you down to make you look up to Him and realize you need Him more than you need anything else. And you need a woman beside you." (Janet)

Me and him, we have really grown. It seems like when men are out on the streets, they want you to listen to them. "Baby, it's like this and that's all there is to it. You don't know what you're talking about." Or even if he knows what you're talking about, they not really, really listening sometimes. That's how my husband is. Now he's in jail, he don't have nothing else to do but listen. And he see where I'm coming from. I met him when I was 17 years old and he was 24, and I was a child to him. . . . When we got together, he acted like I was a dumb little girl: "You listen to me, I know what I'm talking about." But now, since he don't have nothing else to do but listen, I'm letting him know, and wow, "You're really a woman. You know what you're talking about." I'm like, "No, you can't fuck with me." That's the way it is. He listens now. I'm happy he's in jail. He had a reason to rest. 'Cause if he would have been out on the streets, we wouldn't have been together because he don't listen to me. Now, he know me even better. He know me before he went, but it's better now. Our relationship is closer. (Tijuan)

In many cases, communication improves, and a stronger bond and trust emerge.

As far as B___, and he said it himself, which was real hard for him to say, but it's probably the best thing that ever could happen to him. He had had poor experiences with women in the past. . . . He didn't trust anybody. He didn't trust himself. He had an alcohol problem that he's had since he was 15, which he's overpowered himself. . . . This has drawn us closer. That's why he says it's probably the best thing that could have happened to him, 'cause he's learned to trust again. He's learned to trust me and to trust himself, to trust in our relationship. And it does make it difficult at times, having to deal with being able to talk in the visiting room. The phones are difficult because you know there's somebody listening. He's got to put up a tough guy front, they all do. But he has learned how to trust again, and it has helped him a lot. He's gotten his GED, he's gotten into a salable trade. . . . It has helped him and it's helped us. Because had this not happened, he still would have had the stigma of not trusting, where he believes in me now. (Carrie)

Sometimes it seems that I have it a little bit softer in a way because my husband doesn't really get jealous, he doesn't get mad very often or anything. And it's nice because most people I talk to, they tell their husbands that they want to go to the beach, and their husband will get upset and "Why do you want to go there?" Because they have no control over what their wives or girlfriends do. And a lot of them have girlfriends that decide to go to the beach and they decide to talk to this guy or that. Where my husband is always telling me, "Well, why don't you go to the beach, why don't you do that?" So I always feel really different about that. I've noticed that most of them, even now, they always want to go ahead and live their own life even though they are more or less having to serve time with their husband. (Cyndi)

JEALOUSY

The problem of greatest tension centers around jealousy. While not unique to marriages involving prisoners, the fact that the prisoner is not in the home creates his need for extra reassurance. If the wife does something fun, the prisoner sometimes feels angry (Rollo & Adams, 1987). Sometimes if the wife makes a necessary outing, such as to the store or to the doctor's office, the husband feels it is "social" and a neglect of him (Oliver, 1983).

The greatest fear is that the wife will tire of the situation and leave the man to serve his sentence alone, with no caring and no connection to the outside world. Reading in the newspaper of wives "carrying on" in their husbands' absences doesn't help. For instance, divorce rates skyrocketed when soldiers returned from the Persian Gulf. According to one newspaper account, "Breakups are blamed on cheating spouses, depleted bank accounts, overextended credit cards, disputes about who's in charge, and the stresses and strains of recoupling after an extended absence" (Dvorchak, 1991). Many prisoners manufacture scenarios in their heads about the possible interests their wives may have, thus creating instability in their relationships.

Before I got married to him, he wasn't tracking me down a lot. Now, if I'm over at my mom's house, he'll call his mother and have them call over there or he'll want me to leave a phone number wherever I'm at, so he'll be able to talk to me. He wants to know where I've been all the time, what time did I come home. And I feel like he shouldn't ask me that. He should ask me that when he's out taking care of me or something like that. Sometime I don't like for him to ask me, "Where you been?" The whole time he's accusing me of different guys, mainly of my son's father. He just insists on my being with him for some reason. He's always saying when he calls, "Tell that guy you're talking to me now, he have to wait." And I'm like, "What guy? He must be invisible, because he's not in here with me." So, I go through all that. It's just funny sometime. I find myself alone and just laughing to myself about things he say. Like one time he called, and I guess he thought I had on high-heel shoes. He said, "I know you're going to go out, 'cause I hear those high heel shoes. I know you're going out, and I don't want you to wear tight pants." Tight pants, you know. A lot of things have changed since we've been married. He's more or less insecure, that's what he is, insecure. (Sharon)

Jealousy is what's changed. Before, he would have his lady friends and I would know of his lady friends, and I would have my men friends and he would know of my men friends. Then he didn't object as much. But now it's like, "Why did they want to do this?" . . . It's him being jealous and he has doubts. The main thing I understood is he's going to have doubts until he come home. That's no problem. I feel that I'm strong, and I'm willing to try in every way that I can to prove myself to him. And that's mostly what I'm doing most of the time, is proving myself. (Wanda)

When we're in there [visiting], they're selfish. They think they're the only ones who can get hurt and we can't. They think that you can do anything you want to out here, and they're the ones who have to suffer for it because they are sitting in there and they can't do anything. And they don't want you to have fun if they can't have fun. . . . [But] when we're out here and they're in there, we wouldn't hurt them at all. No way. We live for them and that's it. And it's hard for them to believe that. They can think, "I'm in here, somebody else can come along and snatch you right up." (Cathy)

I've known women who mess around, inmates' wives. I can't relate to that at all. I can't comprehend it and I can't accept it. We had one lady living here who was going out on her husband, and we were getting flack from him. He was calling us to find out what's going on, he's got the chaplain calling us to find out what was going on. And she's still visiting with him, and finally we say, "We can't deal with this, we can't deal with the problems you are causing us." Because then our husbands would think, what are we doing that everybody is covering for us? And none of us were that way, so it brought up some more problems for us to deal with. So it had to be changed, she had to go. She couldn't stay in the household because it posed that question for all of them. (Carrie)

Incarceration is a shock, a loss of the familiar routine, and it brings dramatic change and need for adjustment for both the husband on the inside and the wife on the outside. It tugs at insecurities, and while both need reassurance and support for their adaptation, the bulk of the responsibility for maintaining the relationship falls on the woman (Koenig, 1985). No matter how few resources the wife has, she is still the one with the greater resources and the freedom of movement. As Fishman (1990) found in her study, the men feel they need someone in their corner, while the women feel their love can save their men. The husbands appeal to these beliefs by telling wives that no one ever cared before and by getting them to repeat constant reassurances.

He's changed, for one thing. 'Cause he was an alcoholic, is an alcoholic, and he doesn't drink anymore. He had never been in any trouble, and this was really a traumatic way to get in some. And he had a nervous breakdown. Even in jail down in S___ he went through a really rough time. Tried to commit suicide. So, emotionally it's been a very hard, draining time. He always needs to be supported. He gets very depressed and he always needs a lot of encouragement for everything. (Betty)

K___'s mellowed out a lot. He's a lot more kinder, he's not so selfish no more, not so self-centered as he was. Before he used to think only of himself. Now, he doesn't think that way, he thinks of me and D___ and how will everything affect us, not how it is affecting him. "If I have to stay in the hole, I'll go crazy, they're not going to know what to do." He knows how attached we are to him. He knows how attached our baby is to him. He knows if we're all right, he'll be all right, as long as we can be there. One thing he was worried most of all, besides us being all right, is that we might not stick around because it was so hard. But I said, "Hell, this is nothing." That's what I used to tell him, trying to cheer him up. He said, "Honey, I'm so afraid you're going to leave me in this." I said, "Hey, this is nothing." You have to joke with him. We keep each other up. I know we'll make it. When he gets out, he's going to be better. That's what we tell each other, it's going to be a lot better. It's hell, but there's a lot of wives going through hell like this. (Cathy)

COMMUNICATION

The relationships go through a lot of downs with few ups, but something holds them together. Sometimes it's the commitment of the already developed relationship, sometimes truly trying to make a difference in someone's life to help them turn around. A prisoner's wife interviewed by Hurst (1983, p. 34) said, "You figure we're in a situation where most of the time we have nothing to do but talk. Very few married couples have that. And we talk so much of our relationship that we know each other more than a lot of people that have been married 20 years." Women interviewed by Koenig (1985) stated that in many hours of visiting, conversation could be very meaningful, but that it could also be boring and unreal. Communication was often cited by the wives in this study as a key element in keeping the relationship going through the stressful days, months, and years.

[It's important to] keep the communication lines open. To me that's very, very important, and that's what I had to stress to him about writing. I said especially during lockdown. That's when I used to get pissed at him, was during lockdown situations and he wouldn't even write. He was on lockdown once almost two months, that one time 'cause all the Chicano were locked down, and that was very stressful for me because he wasn't writing or anything, and it broke down a lot of the communication. After I said everything I had to say, he realized that it was true. (Cynthia)

A lot of times I get so much pressure on me from when I was working 13 hours a day, 6 days a week, before I changed to this job. It got to me sometimes. And a lot of times I've come down here and I've cried on his shoulder and then tried to hide the tears. 'Cause I think we all do at times. And sometimes, just talking and all of a sudden we just look at each other and . . . tears. It gets like that. Especially when you need them and they're so far away. I write to him or tell him, "If you could just hold me." (Jean)

While the men tend to want to know the details about their wives' lives, they do not divulge much about their lives on the inside. Since the women are accepting of this, some topics are omitted in conversation. Some men will tell their wives significant information about life inside, but not the content of their day-to-day lives. Husbands emphasize, and wives accept, that the inside is just too ugly to relate. One prisoner, writing in *The California Prisoner*, stated it would be impossible to describe life on the inside so someone out of the experience could understand it. Telling of boredom, noise, lack of privacy, stress, and hostility could never adequately convey the experience (Toth, 1985).

I do share some outside problems, pressures, and decisions with J___. Mostly major things. But to be honest, sometimes I just forget, because since he's been gone, I'm just used to making my own decisions, facing my own problems. J___ also only mentions major things as well, even though I prefer knowing everything. But he really only shares things that affect our relationship directly, like visiting, family visits, his job, and things of that nature. (Charlene)

No, he doesn't [share]. I'm curious and I'm always asking. I want to hear stories. People tell me things about him, but he won't tell me 'cause he says it's ugly. He says, "You don't need to know it." If something's real important that needs to get done, he'll tell me, "You have to do this." (Marilyn)

Similarly, wives may not want to burden their husbands with some problems when they know the husband has many problems inside. Wives may have a mixture of emotions they keep to themselves, such as grief, loneliness, and guilt, as well as pride and personal accomplishment (Sommers & Shields, 1987). Some women get used to decision-making and truly forget to discuss everything with their husbands.

Before, I had not fully discussed certain aspects of my life with him because I don't want him worried in there. I try to go in there with a smiling face and everything. That's wrong, though, because marriage is based on communication, and if he feels bad about it, he feels bad about it. I know that there's nothing he can do, but just the fact of talking to your husband is better than keeping it to yourself. (Terri)

He wants to be in my decisions, the important decisions. Something very important to him [would be like] my mother, "Tijuan, I want the little baby to come stay with me for two months in L___." Now that's something me and him will talk about. "Well, my mother wants to take D___ to L___ for two months, what do you think?" "I don't know, Tijuan. I'm already away from home, I feel like you bringing him up to see me." But school, anything beneficial to myself, something that I want to do, I don't even allow him to say no or nothing like that. Tell me I can't work, tell me I can't go to school, I don't want to hear none of that. If anything happened to him, I don't want to be depending on him. What if he die or anything? . . . You know how most men are, "I don't want you working, you stay home and take care of the family." I believe women are supposed to [work]. This is equal rights nowadays. (Tijuan)

Fishman (1990) found that women often want to include their husbands in decision-making so that they can reassert the husbands' dominance and their wifely submissiveness. This could help to neutralize the men's status of prisoner and loss of control on the inside while they continue their family role. However, the wives were selective about what they shared with their husbands. Some withheld information, such as about finances, about which the men would be powerless to do anything.

Communication can help the husband and wife to cope with the reality of two different worlds with differing experiences. One difference is the limitations the men have on the inside. Another is the restrictions the women feel in terms of interacting with their husbands. As Morris (1965) points out, the sense of isolation from the prison world can sometimes be greater for the family than the isolation the prisoner feels. The prisoner has media outlets and the experience of being on the outside, while the family has only visits in the visiting room.

He's in a world I totally can't understand, and the longer he stays in there, he's beginning not to understand mine. Which is kind of hard because, like, when he does call, he asks, "What are you doing?" "Oh, I was going to hop over to Gemco and get da-da-da." He thinks it sounds so strange to get into a car and go someplace. And it's only been a year, and it's hard for him to fathom that, and that's kind of bizarre thinking that. How can you not imagine just going down to the store? Little things like that make me feel bad. (Marie)

I deal with it from the morning phone call until the afternoon mail delivery, and then from the afternoon mail delivery until the morning phone call. And from one weekend visit to the next weekend visit. And I never look too far ahead. Because I found out that you can't. You can't count on it. If he tells me, "I wrote you a letter a week ago and you should have it by now," I may or may not, because they may still be holding it in there. And if he says, "I'll call you tomorrow," he may or may not, because he may be locked down tomorrow. And so I try not to count on anything because it may not happen. (Isabel)

DOING HARD TIME

Being in a relationship can also make doing time more difficult. Having something you care about—perhaps more than anything else in the world—such as a marriage, means the prisoner also has something to lose. This is referred to as doing "hard time." When the prisoner is alone, there are fewer consequences to transfers, or disciplinary actions such as going to the hole or losing visiting or phone privileges. But when a prisoner has a family he wants to see, guards know he won't be as quick to respond to intimidation. The guards can single out the married prisoner to enforce rules, knowing he cannot respond for fear of losing conjugal visits and so forth (Hartman & Cronk, 1988). These are internal stresses the wife may not understand.

IMPACT ON CHILDREN

It is not only the husband and wife who experience a change in their relationship. The children also feel the loss of the father at home, have to visit their father at the prison, and feel the impact of a changed relationship with their mother as she tries to cope and keep the family together. Wives of prisoners and of military men feel a great responsibility to be both mother and father to their children. Sailors' wives reported this was too much for one person (Rosenfeld et al., 1973). Women in Koenig's study (1985) reported being torn between spending time with their husbands and time with their children. Sometimes the husband was not the children's natural father, but he was still treated as the father figure in the family unit. Bringing the children on visits was important, but visiting rooms were not children-friendly areas.

Wallerstein and Kelly (1980) note that during parental separation, children are focused on the disruption to the family unit and worry about what is going to happen to them. Families in which there is divorce face many circumstances similar to those of families facing a father's incarceration. Parents have trouble telling children of the impending separation, visitation is usually stressful, and the loss of one parent in the household is traumatic. Schneller (1976) discovered in his study that children of prisoners were less lonely than their mothers, but they missed their fathers even more than their mothers did.

I feel guilty a lot because a lot of my attention isn't put into where it should be, 'cause I hate to bring her to this place. I hate it. And you saw how long I never ever brought her. But then I started feeling guilty because I wanted to be with her and be here at the same time, and I couldn't do both unless I brought her. So I finally got to the point in my own mind, I said, "OK, I'm going to bring her." . . . Because I don't want her to get involved with people that "this is prison," I don't want her to know it. She doesn't have to. She's not at an age where she has to. (Cynthia)

[They say,] "Can we buy him that? Can't we bring him home?" All of this is common, I'm sure. Or, "When is he coming home?" The older my children get, the less I want them to be in this atmosphere. I think I'm going to keep them away more often. They're very bored and very tuned in to what's going on. I think they see things that they wouldn't imagine that he and I would do in public, or would even do on a family visit, in front of them. And they see it happening in there. It's a little shocking. [They see] lack of respect for each other. Some of the swearing situations. I don't like them to hear people talk to each other that way. (Pat)

Up until recently, it seemed like it didn't affect her at all. But since she's getting older, she has begun to recognize and desire the presence and emotional support of her father. She asks about him daily. Sometimes the first thing she says when she opens her eyes in the morning is, "Mommy, I want to see my daddy. I want to see him now." What hurts me most is that she's always asking when is her daddy going to come home and be with her. All I can tell her is the truth, and that is I really don't know, but it might be soon if God wills. (Charlene)

The age of the child, the previous relationship with the father or stepfather, and changed family circumstances will all affect how the child reacts to the incarceration. Children have their own coping mechanisms. Older children can decide on their own whether to visit the prison, while younger ones feel the tug of wanting to see their dad but hating the boredom of the visiting room. There is no separate play area for children in the visiting room, and playing loudly and running are prohibited. Parents are expected to keep a close watch on their children, so that they don't disrupt other people's visits. Some children pour their energies into school and do well, while others begin to perform poorly, and may worry about classmates finding out their dad is in prison. The children miss doing activities with their fathers, and even a simple task of getting help with homework is usually forbidden when guards won't allow schoolbooks into the visiting room.

The children may be ashamed that their father is absent or they may be confused about the crime their father has committed. Many parents try to explain it in terms they can understand, but that may not ease their questions and concerns about their father's well-being (Hairston, 1988b; Hinds, 1980; Wallerstein & Kelly, 1980).

My older daughter just went away from it, whereas my little girl can't and doesn't want to. She wants to be with daddy. . . . She knows why her daddy is in there. And we tell her he went in because he had drugs on him. And we tell her, "See how much trouble that person can get into? Not only that, but if you do them, it will turn you into a totally different person, ugly." Try to explain it to her like that. She understands. She's pretty smart, so she catches on. (Cathy)

The moving is difficult for them. Then they have to change schools all the time. [My older daughter] was going to a year-round school in S___ and she was doing excellently there. The move was difficult. The change of the people, the race change, she's a minority [here]. But the kids have a good rapport with most of the officers, even. They know the rules and they abide by them. (Carrie)

At school, they will not talk to any of the kids. Like if someone says, "Where's your dad?" and stuff like that, and the oldest one is real, real sensitive, and it really bothers him the most. And he's always saying, "Mom, don't tell anybody, don't tell any of the parents." He's real ashamed. He really loves R___, but he's very ashamed that his dad's in prison. He's [afraid of what] all the kids will say, and I don't blame him, because there's a lot of people who I still can't tell. Especially if I told them what for. . . . But C___ has the attitude like he just does not like people to know. And the younger one, not as bad. He's a little more carefree. He's sensitive, but he doesn't mind telling. (Sue)

LONELINESS

The most common and deeply felt sense of loneliness among the wives is missing their mate to talk with, to do things together, and to feel the bond and presence of someone with whom they share life. Weiss (1974b) writes that loneliness occurs commonly when emotional life isn't shared. Most wives feel that sexual longing is secondary to the missed life-sharing. These were, as Koenig (1985, p. 85) put it, "separate subjects." Loneliness is keenly felt, especially when the wife has no or few friends to whom she can turn, or when the reminders of everyday life reveal a couples' world of which she isn't a part. Depression and jealousy of other couples have been noted in sailors' families as well (Rosenfeld et al., 1973). Oliver (1983) comments that some caregivers of ill partners feel "de-sexed" due to the absence of their partners, especially in comparison with their friends who carry on an active social life. While crying and depression are common, a reluctant and realistic acceptance diminishes the crying as time goes on.

Well, we're incarcerated. I think that we are, the three of us living here. It's almost like solitary confinement. We're not in prison, but they have it easier than we do as far as food, and housing, and clothing. We don't even have that. It's incredible, not to be able to do anything or have anything. And then be separated, too. I wish I was in there with him. I would really live there. I think it would be cheaper, I think if you have family situations. It's not for everybody, I'm saying your A-1 custody [prisoners who work or go to school, have no disciplinary infractions, and retain all privileges]. I think you'd find an institution that would cost half as much to run. You could have general stores and everything. You still have them on AFDC [Aid to Families with Dependent Children] for the family, but they could go to work, the wives. The inmates certainly wouldn't be having their fights because they wouldn't be out, they'd be with their family. You can't describe the loneliness, not to anybody. It's impossible. (Colleen)

[After my first family visit,] I didn't go back into the visiting room. I went home. I said, "I'm not going to cry," and I kept right on going. But then I picked up my mail when I got home, and I had a letter from him waiting for me. And I walked in the house and I just broke down and cried. I just couldn't stop because then I really knew he wasn't there. (JoAnna)

When I'm watching people around me being with their husbands and get to do just simple stuff that I never got to do with him, like have coffee together, go to the store, share some responsibilities, although that's not the main part. The things I miss most are laying in bed, talking. It's the closeness more than any other thing. I just talk to kids, and I'm going crazy. I sleep with kids, talk to kids, take care of the kids, and any other conversations I have, I do have people to talk to around here. I'm not lonely per se, but I am lonely for my partner. (Marilyn)

Compared with loneliness, sexual longing is more variable (Weiss, 1979). For some couples, the desire for physical closeness outweighs any embarrassment they may feel from public display of affection in the visiting room (Koenig, 1985). But for most couples, family visiting is the major relief for sexual contact. The women can plan and look forward to the intimacy of two nights together, whether once a month or every three months. It is not the sex so much as the physical closeness they miss, though some women admit to sexual frustrations and not having a normal relationship in that regard.

Sexually, it's quite hard. I was used to, when we were living together, every day. Then it started out when he was in County, being apart a lot of nights, nothing, no contact, not even holding hands. Well, when we got married, they did let us hold hands and they allowed one kiss. Normal people don't go through that. And normal people, even if they don't have a boyfriend, then they can go out and find someone. J___ once told me if I wanted to, I could. But I don't think it would be the same. I don't think that's something that I would want. (Cyndi)

I know it's hard to believe, but it doesn't bother me not to have any sex. The only time it does bother me not to have any is when he's nearby. Other than that, I don't think about it. It's the farthest thing. All I'm worried about is what is the kid going to eat, what am I going to wear tomorrow, what am I going to do tomorrow, and I got such a short day in my life as it is. The rest of it is his, is where we spend as a family together. (Cathy)

Sexual needs is no problem. I've never really been sexual, sexual aroused. I don't have no feelings for nobody else to want to have sex with them. When it's time for my family visits, I got myself going where we're on standby every month, I'm going to go and have sex with him. And then during that month, that time of month, that's when I want him. 'Cause I know it's coming. But if it's not going to come, I don't sit there and like, "Oh, oh, I need sex. I gotta go and get somebody if I can't find him." I've never been like that. I love him. I can't have sex with anybody I don't love. (Tijuan)

And sexually, yeah, it's frustrating, very frustrating. Not even just the sexual part, but going to bed and knowing somebody's there, it's a lot. I'm sure you know it's a much more comfortable feeling. It's like a part of you is missing. And until he's home, I'll always feel like that, no matter what I do. That will always be there. (Cynthia)

FUTURE PLANS

Dreams of the future can be either exciting or depressing to the wife and husband, depending on the sentence length, the problems incarceration is posing, and the level of adaptation to the situation. Most wives want to have a certain level of security for the family before the prisoner comes home. They don't want him to be faced with a lot of pressures and demands immediately, for fear that he might break under them and revert to the old lifestyle. They hope for certain comforts, such as a car, a TV, and a nicely furnished apartment of their own. They don't want to have money hassles while he is looking for a job. Some dreams include children, some a family business, others simply being together. The process of being optimistic about the future bonds the couple closer, and there is a certain urgency in planning for the future.

I feel like we're just going to begin our lives when he comes home. Like now, we're just waiting to start our lives. And I feel like we're already way behind because we're in our thirties and have babies, instead of having our kids when we were younger. It's so hard to survive anyway, and we have to put if off. So I hope we'll be able to do his parole 'cause it's hard to do parole. But we have a real plan. I feel, his family feels, like he's turned over a new leaf, that he really wants a life outside of being in trouble, that he really wants to raise these kids and really wants to have a life. He feels like he's wasted his life up until now. (Marilyn)

My dreams and my hopes and my goals, of both of us, it's like one, opening our own little business. Just working. He's got brains and I love to work, so let's put it together and do something. He's got those goals. We might move out of town, something to start out fresh. And nobody else saying, "They ain't gonna make it." When we come back, we've made it, and have our own little thing going, our family, going to school, especially our girls going to school. We want to look out for them, have something going for them. (Minerva)

I don't want much, I just want to be with him, be together and share happy times, build a life together. That's all I want, I don't care about anything else. I care about goals. I'd like us to get a house, but I want us to build our own house. I want everything we do to be together, everything. Even little things. To me, that would make me happy. That's all I want. (Cynthia)

Chapter 5

Family Finances

My last phone bill was $135. . . . But I want him to call me every day. I want that. I want to know that he's OK. Every day I want to know that he's OK. (JoAnna)

And he went in and I got stuck with house payments of $750 per month. All I did was work to pay rent and pay bills. Finally I had to let the house go because it was too much for me. And also coming up here every week. My car and gas bill, all that. Then I got laid off from work. I've been on unemployment since October, November. Moved to Soledad 'cause I did lose my house, my job. I lost my car after that. (Minerva)

The wife of a prisoner is faced with handling the financial responsibility and decision making for the family by herself. Along with similar concerns of other wives, she has unique concerns that others do not share. While her husband is limited in his ability to interact with the outside world, she becomes the family's standard-bearer. The wife will be the only wage earner in the family, or she may be on welfare or unemployment. Besides losing the economic contribution of her husband, a wife may lose her job due to the stigma of being married to a prisoner. One woman interviewed by L. Smith (1987) was fired from her job as a nurse. Her income dropped by half when all she could find were part-time jobs.

In this study, 64 percent of the wives worked (not all full-time, however), and one (4 percent) was looking for work. Sixteen percent were on welfare, and one (4 percent) received Social Security for her children. One woman (4 percent) was living off savings, and 8 percent were on unemployment.

SINGLE PARENT INCOME

The financial situation of the prisoner's wife is similar to that of the separated or divorced woman. Generally when a couple separates, the man's standard of living rises while the woman's standard of living decreases. Spanier and Casto (1979) found that women are significantly worse off. With few marketable skills, they have trouble finding a good job, and if children are present, arranging for child care that is affordable is virtually impossible. According to Weitzman (1985), the ex-husband's standard of living rises 42 percent, while that of the ex-wife and children falls 73 percent. Arendell (1986) reports that working married wives contribute less than one-fourth of the average family's income. The superior earning potential of men means that while one out of every nine families headed by a single father is in poverty, one out of three female-headed families is in poverty. These are the same economic realities for the wife who is a single head of the family because her husband is in prison.

In his study, Schneller (1976) found that 56 of the 93 wives reported a decrease in income, with 46 saying it had decreased a great deal. Twenty women reported an increase in income. Interestingly, these women had husbands who had not been contributing to the family income, and their imprisonment meant that now the women were eligible for AFDC or their own incomes were more reliable than their husbands' had been.

Does incarceration of the husband/father result in family crisis? Hill (1949, p. 9) notes three variables that determine whether an event will become a crisis for any given family. First, there are the hardships of the situation or event itself; second, the resources of the family, its role structure, flexibility, and previous history with crisis; and third, the family's definition of the event. Virtually every family in this study reported finances as a problem for them, ranging from very serious, where they could not pay all their bills, to inconvenience in having to rearrange their budgets and plan for the new expenses with a lower income.

Incarceration is interpreted as an environmental stress, according to Dill and Feld (1982). The social environment includes stigma, single parenting, financial burden, visiting stresses, and so forth. In addition to help from their families, the wives coped with the prison system and their husbands' absence primarily through continual contact with their husbands and social support of other prisoners' wives (Carlson & Cervera, 1991). This coping mechanism resulted in increased financial burden; however, it was viewed by them as absolutely necessary. The money stress these wives faced, while not welcome, was seen as something they just had to accept.

The costs of visiting at the prison include money for transportation, food, and possibly overnight housing. Phone calls can only be made collect from the prison, resulting in extraordinarily high phone bills. The wife may be sending stamps to her husband to facilitate his letter writing. Four times a year a package can be sent to supply prison-approved clothing, food, and personal items. Many wives put money into their husbands' account ("on their books") so they can purchase items from the prison-run canteen. Family visiting entails traveling with an ice chest with food for the weekend, clothing, and toiletries.

COST OF VISITING

Thirty-two percent of the women in this study visited their husbands every day or almost every day. Twelve percent visited once a week, and 8 percent visited two or three times a week. Forty percent visited once every other week. One woman (4 percent), visited once a month, and another woman visited once every three months. Visiting involves driving, getting a ride, taking the bus, or sometimes flying. The expense of gas or a ticket is a necessity that the women were always trying to minimize by finding rides with other women, buying a more fuel-efficient car, or moving closer to the prison to shorten travel time and save gas. Similarly, lodging was a concern. Like many prisons, Soledad is located on a remote stretch of a highway. Women shared rooms in the few area motels to save money or stayed overnight at the Friends Outside hospitality house in Salinas. It cost $10 a night for an adult and $3 for children at Friends Outside. For $1 each way, Friends Outside provides transportation to the prison in the morning and back to the house at night. This is a valuable service for the women, making a difficult trip easier. There are also cooking facilities at the house, so women and their children can cook breakfast and other meals there.

Another visiting expense is the food from the vending machines inside the visiting room. Some small meals (such as salads, burritos and rice, or chicken), sodas, snacks, coffee, and cigarettes are available, but the prices are typically quite expensive. However, the only alternative is not to eat, which is not considered an option by most visitors. They pay the inflated prices as part of the costs of visiting their loved ones. In addition, choosing food from the machines is one of the few activities to engage in during a visit.

The costs of visiting, of course, are only part of the total visiting picture. Length of travel time, time spent waiting to get into the visiting room and then waiting for the prisoner to come in, noise, cigarette smoke, and lack of privacy are all aspects of visiting that cannot be quantified. However, as one wife (Terri) states, "My visits to him are the most important thing in my life. I look forward to it every week, and so I guess you could say I put back more now so that I can go do that." Another wife echoes this priority:

It costs at least $150–$200 a trip. I usually come by myself. . . . There are a lot of things that I would like to do. But, I figure this is more important right now 'cause material things come and go. I can get them anytime. And as far as I'm concerned, I'd rather start all over with all that stuff when he gets out anyway. It would be "ours." It is frustrating sometimes, it is, to think of all this money that's being wasted. But to me, it's not wasted, because to me it's what I want to keep the communication lines open. (Cynthia)

This is what women who travel far and stay overnight spend:

It takes about $30 round-trip for the gas. It was costing me a little over $25 for the night for the motel. The people at the motel were very nice and gave me a break because I'm a regular customer, so it's down to $20 a night for the motel. Plus, I don't eat that much for myself on the outside. I eat junk food, cheap junk food. But then there's another few dollars every day on the inside for R___ and I to eat. . . . I spend about $80–$100 a weekend. (Isabel)

So, financially, to come up here because it is so far, it's just really very, very hard with the money. Before I started coming up with my friend, it was running me $103 for a bus ticket, $40 for a hotel room, and then food in the visiting room, which usually runs $30–$40. So it was a good $200 just to come up for a weekend. Which, needless to say, I could not afford. Sometimes I would come up here with his family, and it would be cheaper that way because we would share the gas expense, but they didn't come as often as I wanted to come. Now, it runs anywhere from $50 to $75. (Betty)

The bus tickets are $32.50 round-trip. I could go down there with $50 and be comfortable. Sometimes I stay at Friends Outside. It depends on if my money's right, it depends on what time of the month I go. If it's the middle of the month, I stay at Friends Outside. But sometimes I go just for the day. The bus gets down there at 9:30 in the morning, and I stay till 8 P.M. . . . which means I don't get home until 7:00 Monday morning. Without having a car it's hard. (Janet)

When wives live closer, such as in the town of Soledad or in Salinas, they visit more frequently.

If you figure, on average, if I went in every day, I was spending about $10 per day with him and the two kids. That's when [my older daughter] was here. We rarely ate here at home. We ate there with him. So you figure the cost of living wasn't too high with food or anything. We didn't have to visit too long. Then we would visit from 6 to 9 when he first came here, when he worked. So, we had all day to do nothing. . . . But when it was [visiting] all day long, it was $20 or $25. It was quite a bit of money. And then the gas you put in your car to go there. Then something happens to your car, which is being used a lot more. (Cathy)

We figured out that we spend $10 a day in visiting for food, and visiting five times a week. We've budgeted ourselves pretty much. We try to keep it down to $5 a day. When I was in Salinas, I was coming down quite often, and that was when I had my Camaro. It was about $10 a day in gas. I got rid of the Camaro, and now I have a Datsun. With living closer, it's less. (Cyndi)

COST OF PHONE CALLS

While visiting occurs once a week or every few weeks for most wives, phone calls are more frequent and become the major expense. Again, the price paid is seen as worth it in order to maintain the relationship and be reassured that their husband is all right. Keve (1974) points out that we take availability of phones and privacy for granted. For the prisoner, privacy is lost because guards listen in on phone lines. Phone calls must be made collect by the prisoner, who does not always have access to a phone when he wants or when it is convenient to reach his wife. During lockdowns, no phone calls are allowed. Of the participants in the study, 24 percent of the respondents spoke to their husbands every day. One wife (4 percent) spoke three to five times a week, and 12 percent spoke two or three times a week. Eight percent spoke once a week. One (4 percent) spoke two or three times a month, and 40 percent rarely or never spoke on the phone. Eight percent reported phone calls but did not mention the frequency of calls.

R___ was calling me more often, but he stopped because I told him what the bill was, and he couldn't believe it. It averages $75 to $100 a month. So he stopped it. It's just been a few months that he's cut down. He's more worried about the bills than I am. (Sue)

I spend money on nothing other than necessities. Things that I used to do, I no longer do so that I will have the money to pay the phone bill and come up here. Last month [the phone bill] was $129, and he was locked down for two weeks out of the four. Without lockdowns, it would have been double that. (Isabel)

[We talk on the phone] $239 worth! I talk to him sometimes every night, two and three calls a night. . . . I told him he can't have his cake and eat it, too. I asked him, "Would you rather have money on your books or the telephone bill?" He kept calling, and that answered the question for him. (Sharon)

I know that some people, they call and talk all day. You can't do that, because that means money coming out of your pocketbook when you could be putting it on their books. And keeping the phone bill up [or the] phone gets cut off, no, that doesn't work. (Janet)

LETTER WRITING

Another important means of communication is writing letters and sending cards. Wives tend to write more than the husbands. Thirty-eight percent of the respondents wrote every day or almost every day. Another thirty-eight percent wrote two or three times a week. Seventeen percent wrote once in awhile. Eight percent sent cards rather than letters. It is not unusual for the wife to send her husband stamps to avoid that cost being deducted from his account. That expense, then, is similar to her sending money, and has the advantage of encouraging him to write.

SENDING PACKAGES

Four times a year, eligible prisoners may receive a package containing approved clothing (jeans, sneakers, pajamas, undergarments), canned foods (meats, salsa, coffee), snacks (sealed chips, raisins, crackers), and items like playing cards, cigarettes, and stationery. Quantities are limited, colors are limited, and everything must be factory sealed. No glass containers can be sent. For the prisoner, it becomes the only variety from the canteen-purchased items. Furthermore, it is the only time prisoners can receive items or gifts from personal friends or family other than direct from vendors. It is the true "CARE package."

The packages cost from $100 to $300, and represent a burden for many prisoners' families. But wives say they want to send them and make their husbands as comfortable as possible under the circumstances. Wives in Fishman's study (1990) claimed that they wanted to give their husbands clothes, food, television sets, and so forth, but that this nurturing resulted in depriving themselves of what they needed. Scarce resources flowed to the men. Koenig (1985) similarly reported that in taking care of the husbands, wives often had to neglect their children's needs for clothing and activities. Lack of money for child care meant children accompanied their mothers everywhere they went.

The packages are an expression of love and caring to the sender, and a variety and joy in an otherwise mediocre existence to the receiver. When something goes wrong, it becomes a major source of tension. Occasionally packages are lost, either by the Postal service or within the prison. Sometimes a package may sit for days or weeks in the prison office before the prisoner can get to pick it up due to the hours of pickup (which may conflict with work hours) and the need to get a ducat (a pass authorizing movement) to go there. Those decisions are in the hands of prison guards.

Further tension occurs when items in the package don't fit, but the prisoner doesn't know that until he gets back to his cell. The items then cannot be easily sent back to his wife to return or exchange them. Some items are rejected as unauthorized, such as when the packaging is not factory-sealed, there are too many items, the color is wrong, or the item is not on the approved list. In that case, the prisoner is supposed to have the option of sending them back to his family or "donating" them. Sometimes this option isn't given, and the items are donated. But the prisoner does not know where they end up, and often suspects that the guards pocket them.

He's had one package, which cost me a lot of money. Food and clothes. I spent close to $200. I'm preparing now for another package. I buy a little at a time. And right now he's got a TV on layaway that I've been paying on. He's been waiting for that for a long time. I decided to put it on layaway and I could put a little on at a time. (Wanda)

You're talking about one hundred and something dollars right there. Which is no problem because I have a fairly good job. . . . But by the time I'm getting ready to send out a package is the time I had to spend $400 worth of repairs on my Jeep. . . . A lot of times he'll send me a list of things when I can send a package and I thought, "I wonder if he knows how much this is costing?" I don't think he does. And I won't tell him till he gets home, because he'll shorten the list and I don't want that. I want him to have everything that they need. (JoAnna)

I send him packages. That costs $200 a whack. It's expensive. We lost two packages. I don't know if the post office took them or here in Soledad, I really don't. (Cathy)

I send him his packages, and those run me about $150 every three months. So that's an added expense that month. I just know that income isn't coming in, so I've cut back. And the children understand that. (Sue)

HOUSING CONCERNS

Many wives, 40 percent, lived alone or with their children. Twenty-eight percent lived with their parents or other relatives, and another 28 percent lived with roommates, often other prisoners' wives. One wife was in the army and lived on the base.

As a fixed expense, housing becomes a major concern. A woman's housing situation usually changes once the husband is incarcerated or when she meets and marries a man who is already incarcerated. The wives' housing arrangements mirror what Hill (1949) found with military wives: wives moved in with family to save money, to ward off loneliness, and sometimes because the husbands wanted the family to help them and watch out for them.

The only reason we own [our home] is because of family support. We could've never made it without them now. The first couple of years, yes, I could pay all the bills and I could get by. But in order to be close to him, in order not to lose him to the system. . . . I couldn't go to work. There was no way I could keep him as a human being and work. So there's no money left, because our house payments alone were almost $500 a month. It's rented now [and] we live in this squalor. (Colleen)

My kids have Social Security income, and we get by pretty much on that. I'm not working now, and I'm not getting any social benefits, just the Social Security. The incarceration affects spending money because there isn't that much available. It's tight. We have about $780 a month. With rent, utilities, food, etc., there's little left over. That's why we all live together. There's constantly four women living in the house. (Carrie)

I rent from my mother, she has a duplex. She's been my lifesaver. And at Christmas, my daughter moved in with me, so she's taken over the majority of my bills. (Betty)

I've been living here for a year and a half. I live with my husband's sister, her husband, and family. It's beautiful 'cause it's closer to the prison, and I couldn't afford living in S___ anymore, which is where I lived before, and that's where I was working. Once I had my daughter, I couldn't keep working and pay for child care and live in S___. We just felt it would be better for the sake of the children and me and my marriage if I moved here. And it was definitely better 'cause it's supportive. (Marilyn)

I was living in a house by myself and another person, but I was paying everything.

But it's gotten to the point where I'm sharing a home with a woman that's on welfare and paying her $140 a month to have a place to stay. (Vicky)

SUPPORTING TWO BRANCHES OF THE FAMILY

While all families juggle their expenses and make plans in their long-run interests, families of prisoners are concerned with paying their bills on the outside, keeping him as comfortable as possible on the inside, and putting money aside for when he does come home. The woman is the head of the household, making decisions and trying to cope, frequently helping other prisoners' wives.

You don't really know how hard it is until you go through it. Nobody knows the stress, the money you put out and everything. A lot of my money went into food for other women who came here and stayed, that were broke and had no money to eat. And they were sleeping in their cars. We were taking a lot of women like that. . . . I still do it. Why should I stop? I'm used to helping people. It doesn't bother me that the money goes to that, but it does get high. (Cathy)

Before, I always had money in the bank. I've been working and I had my freedom. It's not that I would go anywhere too much, but I would go to church, go here, go there. And I always had money in the bank. And then after I met him, well, they have to have something. Some clothes. I bought his dress-outs. Every time he'd get out, that means dress-outs. New shoes. . . then he needs Levis, sweaters, tennis shoes, socks, you name it. Then they want money to go to the canteen. It gets sort of expensive. I think in five years we've gone over $5,000. (Jean)

The only expenses that have occurred that are pretty great are attorney fees 'cause we're still fighting. We're trying to get a trial granted through the federal courts for civil rights violations. And I also have four lawsuits against Soledad prison right now, which in the last week I put over $5,000 up in attorney fees to represent those. (Misty)

I was working seven days a week, every week. In fact, I did extra work. Our shifts in the clinic were twelve hours on, twelve hours on call, three days on, three days off. So the three days you were on their beck and call the whole time. Well, I would work six days on so I could have six days off every two months, so that somebody else would work my shift and I could go to California. And I had to have money for hotels, motels, rental cars, either gas to get there by car or a plane ticket, food, everything. So I had to have a second job, there was absolutely no way around it or I wouldn't have been able to see my husband. (Jeni)

My situation is that when F___ first got into trouble, I was working, and then I needed neck surgery, and since then I've lost my job. I can't work at all. The only work I do at all is what I do at home. I'm a seamstress. So it doesn't bring in very much money. I'm not able to do too much work. I don't receive any social services. I'm too young, I don't have any children, I'm not old enough to get a lot of the aids that people can get. I haven't worked enough to get Social Security. (Betty)

TENSIONS OVER BUDGETS

As the women are concerned with providing for their husbands, and adjusting their own lifestyles to the new limitations (no new clothes, no luxuries, no extras for the children), their husbands are not always understanding of their stress. Money, as in most relationships, becomes a source of tension. Sometimes it's because the prisoner wants more, but generally he just seems to have lost touch with the high cost of living.

Right now we're kind of feuding because he asked me to send him $50. And there's no way I can do it even though I've just gotten an income tax check. That money is in my savings for when I may need to get groceries real quick or thus and so. He doesn't understand. I know he don't 'cause everything is laid out for him. He don't know what it's like to pay P. G. & E [Pacific Gas & Electric]. He don't know what it's like when people say we want you to pay on this day, and if you don't, they gonna cut it off. (Sharon)

It gets rough, and we get into little arguments because he feels I spend money where I shouldn't spend, and he gets upset because I spend money on him as far as packages go that he doesn't feel he has the right to ask me yet because we're not married. But I feel because I love him and he's in the spot where he's at. . . . Of course he had to do something wrong to get there, but at the same time. . . . So what money I have and can afford, I don't mind putting out. (Vicky)

We fight about it all the time. It's put a strain on our relationship. He doesn't understand where my money goes and why can't I do this and why can't I do that. Why can't I come visit more. He says, "Don't get on me about the phone calls." And "Why can't you buy this for the kids, and why can't you buy this for yourself? I don't understand where your money goes." And I'm on a set income. (Marilyn)

Chapter 6

Visiting at the Prison

The prison system serves its purpose. If a person commits a crime, he must do the time, I agree. But because a person makes a mistake in his/her life doesn't make them less than human. In prison they treat them like animals. I'm in total opposition to that. As for the guards, you run into some who respect you and treat you like you're human, but on the other hand, you run into some who are so programmed into treating inmates like dogs or wild animals that they lose touch with society and start treating visitors like they've committed some type of crime as well. (Charlene)

When I first started coming down, it used to scare me. He'd said be sure to take the bus to North, so I go into Central, "Where do I get the bus to North?" And they look at me like, "You mean you don't know?" They don't explain anything; they expect you to know. And then I get over there and I'm in there, and he must have been curling his mustache or doing something with his hair, and it took him an hour to get out there. I'd never seen him, he didn't have any pictures, so I'm, "What am I doing here? I came down here on the bus, I've no idea where I'm at. I've just gone through this whole rigmarole in here, there are people staring at me." (Laura)

I felt very uncomfortable at first. I was frightened, what's going to happen? Is somebody going to stab somebody or maybe somebody will get shot? 'Cause I never had any experience with anybody with anything like that, and you know what you see in the movies, so that was the first feeling. . . . My understanding of having a visit is to keep the family unit together. But as far as I am concerned, they don't even encourage that at all. If you sit in a room for six hours and you're not allowed to hold hands or kiss or touch, as far as I'm concerned, that's not helping to hold the family together. You should be able to lay your head on his shoulder or hug or be comforted or give comfort. And you're not allowed to do that. If you do do it, then somebody comes in and fusses at you like you're a little child, and they'll take the guys out in the back room, bang them up against the wall. So it's not a very pleasant situation at all. You either have to totally ignore it and get in your own little world, or I imagine it could really upset you quite a bit. (Betty)

While wives and girlfriends try to bring joy and stability to their relationship through visiting, visits themselves can be a tremendous source of anxiety (Koenig, 1985). In addition to the costs, travel time, lodging, and concern with children, conditions within the visiting room and the way guards treat the visitors add to stress. Visitors feel that they fight an uphill battle against the prison system to have a visit that is sincere and without stress. Both families and prisoners spend time preparing for the visit, whether mentally or physically, but once inside the visiting room, the lack of privacy, the lack of activities, the noise and smoke, and too hot or too cold conditions can make a visit unpleasant. At some prisons, during the winter, visitors sit with their coats and gloves on, while in summer it is unbearably hot.

SECURITY VS. REHABILITATION

A visiting program to encourage rehabilitation runs contrary to the safety and security needs of the prison. Meaningful visiting cannot occur in a context of stress and conflict. The lack of privacy, noise, and constant watching by guards in the visiting room can lead to frustration for families rather than contribute to family stability (Goetting, 1982a). The prison rules requiring clearance screenings, metal detectors, searches, picture IDs, limited physical contact, dress codes, and limitations on what you can bring into the visiting room are seen by visitors as blocks to family bonding. What the wives view as harassment, the prison views as necessary to minimize contraband and drug smuggling, and escape possibilities.

The prison administration states that these are not personal rules directed at individuals, but rules mandated by the public for safety and security (B. Burton, interview, May 1, 1991). The wives, however, take these rules personally and feel they are hypocritical. The lack of privacy, in particular, impedes the maintenance of family ties (Fishman, 1990). Many feel that visiting is actively discouraged by prison administrations. The visiting conditions are restrictive and uncomfortable. There are rarely areas for children, there is a lack of waiting areas for visitors in the cold and rain, and the distrustful attitude of guards conveys the unofficial line about visiting, discouraging visitors from returning (Hairston, 1988b; Hedin, 1986). Barriers to visiting cited by Z. Nazeeh (interview, April 5, 1991) include traveling distance, lack of sensitivity on the part of guards, dress codes, and the processing procedure—where, for example, metal detectors are set low enough for a metal clasp on a bra or a hairpin to set them off.

THE VISITING ROOM

The visiting room is, as Rollo and Adams (1987, p. 37) say, an "unnatural place to see your loved one." This setting is a "gigantic container of hostility." But the only way for the women to see their husbands is to come to the prison.

When they try to comfort their husbands, or try to express their love and caring, guards frequently step in and instruct them to stop. It may be to stop holding hands, stop hugging or kissing, or to stop touching knees.

Women in Koenig's study (1985) reported that guards required them to sit at 90 degree angles to one another, with visit cancellation the penalty if that position was changed. Women were sometimes ready to risk visit termination to get closer to their husbands. On the other hand, some families are reluctant to voice their objections to unfair rules or their application for fear of retaliation and loss of visiting privileges (Weinstein, 1989).

A walk around the visiting room at Soledad, after hours of sitting, is approved of, but to stop and lean against the wall for some privacy away from other visiting families will bring forth the command "Get off the wall." A prisoner may be called to the back room and roughed up by a guard who disapproves of his behavior, and visits are terminated if enough "warnings" are given. This close watching and being treated like children is resented by prisoners and their wives. The entire mood of the visiting room can be controlled by the attitude of the guards on duty at that time.

Upon arrival at Soledad (Soledad is a triplex facility, Central, North, and South, divided by security level.), visitors to North need to take a van to the North facility and go through processing there. There are several points of interaction with guards. Overwhelmingly, women complain that guards treat them with much disdain, discourteously, and sometimes in ways that show contempt. The women believe they are looked upon as "guilty by association" with the men they are visiting. Most women in Koenig's study (1985) reported being treated with disrespect and suspicion. One prison chaplain, Father Kane, contrasts the degradation of prison wives with treatment of those visiting loved ones at a hospital or military academy: "It is as if they were put on public display in a negative manner" (Anderson, 1985, p. 259).

And then they're breathing down your neck and back and everything when you want to hold hands or kiss. Sometimes I feel like they should understand the situation. They know we're not seeing each other. Then instead of them making it hard for us, they should more or less make it easy for us. There was a lady officer, she didn't want you to turn toward him, both of you have to be in a straight line, looking straight. (Sharon)

I think we're being punished as much as they are. I think that the system is designed to make it as difficult on us as possible. Because it hurts them inside. It's another way of getting at them, is through us. . . . To have to stand outside and freeze in the cold for three hours to get in, when they're sitting behind the doors in a warm office looking at you. The fact that visiting is supposed to start at nine o'clock in the morning, but they will not even transport us away from here until nine o'clock in the morning, which effectively cuts into our visiting time. The visiting room itself, the conditions are terrible. Sit in there all day with a bunch of machines that don't even work. . . . It's very hard to have an effective visit because there's absolutely no privacy. And there are things I know that R___ would like to say to me that he will not say over a phone because people are standing there listening, that he will not put in a letter because the mail is read. And then he can't say it to me either when we're in there because there's too many people around. And I understand the need for security and such, but I do believe that it should be possible to have a little more privacy for conversation. (Isabel)

For visitors with children, the problems have an additional slant. The children want to see their dad or stepdad, and the men want to see their children. Except for family visits, this is their only time together. But the visiting room lacks space for children to play in, and there is nothing for the family to do together. Furthermore, guards are also arbitrary in their application of rules. One week children can sit on dad's lap, the next week they can't (Weinstein, 1989).

Another thing, it's too closed in. Not enough play area for the kids. There isn't any. They're always constantly threatening you that if you don't settle your kids, you'll get a visit termination. What else can the kids do but be kids? So it's a lot of hassles in there. With the kids, you try to have a good conversation with your spouse, and there's nothing for the kids to do. They disturb you and act like kids. They need something for the kids to do. (Minerva)

Most of the time, I'm very uncomfortable 'cause I'm not the type of person that likes to have a million people around. Things that I want to discuss with him are private. You can't even hear yourself think half the time. To me the closeness just isn't there. I don't like having to be afraid if I hug him too much or show a little affection. I don't like to worry about whether they're watching or whether they're going to come over and say "Don't do that." It's a very uncomfortable feeling. . . . And I don't like having to watch C___, not that I don't want to watch C___, but it's like kids are going to be kids, they're going to play, they're going to run. I feel bad that I have to tell her you cannot run, you cannot do this, you cannot do that, you cannot, cannot, cannot. (Cynthia)

I think that sometimes they should organize little games, like the wives could come on certain days and we could play baseball or something. Or they should have games like checkers or cards that we could play. They figure like these men are getting a visit and they can have touching and all this, that's all they need. They have a tendency to look at them as the crime that they did and not as a human being. They look at them like, oh, they robbed a store and they're a thief, put that thief in a cage. (Tijuan)

VISITING RULES

Most regular visitors encounter some problem among the many things that can go wrong. Sometimes visitors are turned away for clothing that may not be approved. They wear blue denim, their blouse is considered too see-through, their neckline is too low. These determinations vary from guard to guard, so something you wore one week without a problem may be a reason to be turned away at another time. Rules are applied arbitrarily, which creates additional friction among visitors and guards (Koenig, 1985).

If a prisoner wants a visit during his work hours, he needs to be granted an "earned time off" (ETO) by his supervisor. That form must be sent to the visiting room. Many wives arrive to find the ETO form missing. Some guards will call the job supervisor and see if it had in fact been approved, but others will just turn the visitor away to wait until work hours are over. Meanwhile, the prisoner, who has been given the time off from work, is sitting in his cell waiting to be called for the visit.

Other visitors may be turned away if they do not have a picture identification with them, even if they are known by the visiting staff. Out-of-state visitors may be turned away for the same reason, the hours and expense of travel a waste. Other hassles occur in the visiting room, when visits may be terminated for too much touching.

Once when I came to visit on two of his off days, I didn't have a problem on the first even though his counselor forgot to turn in his "Earned Time Off" slip, which they're allowed two of them a month. The visiting officer called his work supervisor, verified that the counselor had okayed them, and I got in with no problem. But the second day was heart-throbbing because the slip was still not sent down in the visiting room, and the sergeant told the visiting officer that if J___'s ETO slip was not in, I could not visit until after work, which was after 1 o'clock, and visiting was over at 3, even if I did come all the way from L___. I explained to him that I was there yesterday and the visiting officer, which was different from the one on this day, had verified it and that's how I visited the previous day. He replied by saying that he refused to allow the officer to call and verify, and he refused to verify it himself. So I sat there looking pitiful right there in their face from 8:30 to 1 o'clock. But to top it off, as I was entering the visiting area where the inmates come out, there was the sergeant coming out as I was coming in. He stopped, looked at his watch and said, "It's after 1:00, huh?" and chuckled at me in a mockery-type laugh. (Charlene)

There are things I get tired of, being in there every week and telling them who I am, can't find his file, or something like that, but it gets very old and they know who you are. And at one point in time I forgot my driver's license [in the car] and everybody there knew me, but I still had to go back and get my driver's license. (Vicky)

They're rude. They humiliate you, making their comments and you're doing nothing in the visiting room. I was cold, I had my coat on. "Take your coat off." "Excuse me?" "I can't tell what you're doing underneath your coat." I said, "I'm sitting here. My husband's hands are by his chair, and mine are on mine." So, they're very humiliating, very degrading. [Another time] my husband had his hand on my back and on my shoulder, and they pulled my husband in the back, and, of course, the whole room saw them take him back, "What did he do? What did he do?" And it was for "too much handling." So that is humiliating to me. (Colleen)

VISITING ROOM GUARDS

The tension that exists between guards and prisoners is reflected in the relationship between guards and visitors. Most visitors are friendly to the guards, especially at first, because they want to make the best of the situation and make it as pleasant as possible. However, given the reality of the situation, that the guards are there to enforce rules, the relationship erodes. Some guards are seen as friendly and easygoing; most are seen as unfair, petty, and power tripping. The guards represent what the prison stands for, and in the interaction during visiting, it is virtually impossible to have positive relations. Women in Fishman's study (1990) felt that interaction with guards repeatedly opened them up to feelings of shame and degradation. The constant distrust erodes their self-esteem.

He especially will not talk to a guard. And I think he gets a little upset because I would talk to them. If I liked one of them, I would talk to them. If somebody's going to be rude and nasty to me, then I won't have anything to do with them. But it doesn't bother me to talk to them. It doesn't mean that I approve of the way that they treat them. I know what they do here. It doesn't mean I really like them, because I don't really know them. But I don't really dislike a lot of them either. . . . I think one of the things W___ does not like is some of the women who will be watching when they're taking a shower, walk in on them when they're on the toilet. They say there's no privacy. Or feeling them down. He's totally against that. He says in a women's prison it shouldn't be men doing this to women, and in a men's prison it shouldn't be the other way around. It just shouldn't be, but it happens. (JoAnna)

I try to keep in mind that they're there to do their job, and they're only human beings. I do not like the feeling I get from them that the women are underdogs or they are lowlifes or that the men are lowlifes. . . . I don't like it. But at the same time, I don't like to let them know that. That's why I just go in there, go through their procedures, go through what they want to do, and I feel instead of bucking their system, it's going to be easier on everyone altogether. But there's a lot of things I don't like the way they handle. (Vicky)

I think more or less the guards' attitude is, "Well, this is prison. Those are the animals. We're paid to take care of them and this is it." And many of the guards think that way, probably the majority of them. But there is a handful that you run into in there that R___ has told me about that are really kind, very good men, and they treat you like a human being. And those are the ones that are very rare, and those are the ones that make the system bearable for R___. (Sue)

I don't worry so much anymore because I've met more of the inmates and I find it's not the inmates that cause most of the problems, it's the guards. . . . I've come across about three guards who have actually been nice, they can be called a person. And the rest of them are mostly very prejudiced. They aren't prejudiced racially, they're prejudiced against inmates and their visitors. The visiting guards are the only ones I've really had contact with, but I find them prejudiced. Just the fact that I'm going in there to see an inmate. (Cyndi)

One situation that arises for many women is that a guard disrespects their marriage. Whether the guard believes the prisoners aren't worthy of this devotion, that the women deserve a better life, or the guard is himself attracted to the wife, the women do not see these comments as friendly or sincere.

You know the biggest question the guards ask me is, "Why the hell would a woman like you marry a guy in prison?" It's like he has some kind of plague, he's a scumbag. He's a reject from society, and why would I subject myself to being with him. . . . They just don't understand, these are people, too. They just made mistakes. (Misty)

And they shouldn't badmouth people . . . I've had several tell me, "You don't deserve this kind of life, tell him 'later' and get out of the situation." I've been told that by guards. One lady guard said, "What you need to do is find an understanding older man" where I could be sexually satisfied and live happy with someone like that, and he'd know about P___, and him understand that situation, but not tell P___. Because all that would do is ruin the relationship. . . . And I don't appreciate guards trying to pick up on you because your husband is down and that you probably get lonely. (Marie)

One time I said, "I can't wait for my family visit." And one of the officers said, "Oh, is that all you're worried about?" I said, "Yeah, that's what I'm worried about." She goes, "You can get that anywhere." I don't need to hear that. I told her, "Hey, I want my husband. I don't want just anything." So I told my husband, he said, "You should have said something stronger. You should have said, 'Hey, I'm not like you,' or something." (Minerva)

Many of the reservations the wives have when dealing with the guards have to do with the brutality that does occur on the inside. There is violence and intimidation, rumors and setups. Behavior of some guards makes all of them suspect.

I was walking through the parking lot on my way to Saturday morning visiting and there's an officer in the car in front of me . . . he was looking in the mirror, and I could tell he was looking at me. He was an O-wing officer, and a couple days prior he had made a threat to R___. He told R___, "You'd better be careful walking around the third tier with handcuffs on. You could fall off." I was sitting there watching him, and I got out of the car and I went to walk by him . . . he was still sitting in the car, and I looked down, and this bumper sticker said, STOP CRIME, SHOOT FIRST. If you look underneath it, in tiny letters it says, Sponsored by the American Vigilante Society. Well, he got really upset because I stopped and I wrote it down. And I wrote his tag number down and kept on walking. So he walked up to the front and he said, "What were you doing?" And I said, "Your bumper sticker, I wrote it down." He said, "Why?" And I said, "Well, obviously you display it, you don't mind if people read it. I just saw the bumper sticker, and I didn't want to forget what it said. Is there a law against that? Don't tell me a pencil's become an illegal weapon on the grounds, too." And he just smirked and walked outside. Well, that afternoon I told a couple of my friends about it inside, so they watched out for me and I cruised the parking lot to the entrance building. I found 22 more of them in the employees' parking lot, and there was seven of the ones with the big gun that say GO AHEAD, MAKE MY DAY. I wrote those down, too. And I wrote to the Department of Corrections, wanting to know why they condone it. I said, "If it was a few bumper stickers, I would have thought the people may have bought them being humorous. But when there was 23 in one small parking lot on one shift, I had to feel that maybe there is an organization that is the American Vigilante Society. Vigilantes are not allowed to be police officers, they're not allowed to serve on juries. They are barred from just about every type of government position." I wanted to know why the Department of Corrections condones it. (Misty)

FAMILY VISITING

California is one of six states that allows family, or conjugal, visiting. The program began in 1968, for the primary purpose of helping family unity and stability. Not all prisoners can participate. Prisoners in SHU (Security Housing Unit), those who refuse to work or participate in a training program, and those who are on noncontact visiting status are not eligible. Burstein (1977) feels that this program humanizes the lives of the prisoners in an environment of severe deprivation. In addition, he feels that the wives (or girlfriends) should not be deprived of their sexual relationships because their partners are in prison. Most states use home furloughs as a means of providing families time together. Fishman and Cassin (1981) point out that many view home furloughs as preferable to family visiting because in addition to strengthening family ties, the prisoner can handle business within the community and carry out more husband and father roles.

The parents, wife, children, and siblings of the prisoner are allowed to visit for two nights with the prisoner in a trailer or small apartment on the grounds of the prison. The prison supplies the bedding, kitchen needs, and a television set. The family brings food, clothing, toiletries, and games or books. There are limits to the number of bags of food and suitcases, and rules on how food is packaged. No electrical appliances or battery-operated toys or radios are allowed. Regardless of the limitations, this is the only truly private time the families have. Prisoners have to appear for count several times a day, but within the trailers, the families are left to themselves.

Families on standby, those called at the last minute when there are cancellations or no-shows, get to visit nearly every month. Regularly scheduled visits come every three months. Prisoners in close custody have family visits every four to six months, mainly because there are few close custody visiting units. These are trailers that are set apart with a barbed wire fence surrounding them. The most common visit is between prisoner and wife, or prisoner, wife, and children. But family visits are also a time for parents to visit their sons in prison.

Family visiting is a common topic of conversation among couples, as they plan their menu, any special activity they may want to do, or just dream about the privacy together. During the family visit, wives feel that sex is just one aspect of their time together (Bloom & Cohen, 1981; Nazeeh, interview, April 5, 1991).

It's strange being inside the prison. If something happened, you can't just walk out. You can't get in your car and leave. That's scary. But at the same time, like sometimes I've gone on visits when I've been really sick. Like one time I got food poisoning on a family visit and he was there. We've had family visits when we've had sex once or twice maybe, but it's mostly just leaning back, talking and holding each other. Sex is nice, but that's the basic part, just being able to talk without having somebody sitting within five feet of you, without a guard walking around looking at you all the time. And being able to go out and play in the yard. We got a roll of toilet paper and played football with it, and we play on the kids' jungle gym a lot. It's nice being able to pretend that you're . . . normal for a little while. I think [family visits] are real important. I think they help keep a semblance of family, help keep the fact that you are still together as man and wife. And for the kids, it's like they still do have a father. I think it helps a lot with the relationship just to be able to talk privately, to just be together, to do . . . things like cooking dinner. To do things that many people who aren't in that position take for granted, like washing dishes, watching TV, having someone walk in on you when you're trying to go to the bathroom. . . . In visiting, you can see each other and feel each other, but it's not quite the same as actually being married where you can be together. (Cyndi)

Because of him being in close B custody, we only have them every four to six months, which is about twice a year. But I must say it's better than no time a year, and it's the only avenue of prison that truly encourages and strengthens family bonds. . . . Our visits are almost like paradise. It definitely strengthens the bond between me and my husband, and my daughter and her dad. On our family visits we're able to give each other our undivided attention without distraction. Family visits make you feel like you're married and not single. (Charlene)

One frequently cited issue is the short amount of time the family has together in terms of adjusting to each other (Nazeeh, interview, April 5, 1991). Seamen and their wives felt similarly that the time on leave was not adequate to allow for a gradual transition and adjustment to family life (Rosenfeld et al., 1973).

We usually have a fight, maybe two, because it's like you have to adjust to living with them and you have to do it so fast, because you're only there not even two days. And you go through all these emotions, and so naturally you're going to fight a little more often than if you were home and you knew, "Oh, he's here, I have all the time in the world to talk to him, to know how he feels." You get so excited, and then it's for such a short time, you don't have any time to prepare yourself for it being over. So that's hard. (Laura)

LACK OF INFORMATION

A major complaint of the women is the lack of information given by the prison to the visitors, the inconsistency of rules, and the contempt in which guards seem to hold visitors trying to get information. "Knowledge is power" has never been more true than in a system such as this. Even when signs are posted regarding contraband, visitors are not always sure what constitutes contraband. Are pictures, toys, or food contraband (Koenig, 1985)?

I understand why they don't tell the family in advance where they are going [to be transferred] because they could try to find an escape, but they should at least have the information where that person is when they call. We went all the way up to Vacaville, and they had no idea where he went. . . . And how do you know not to wear jeans down there? You don't know every inmate wears jeans. How do you know that you don't get picked up [by the van] between four and six [o'clock] because of count? [At 4 P.M. all movement into or out of the prison stops while they count the prisoners. Thus, visitors arriving around 4 P.M. do not get picked up by the van for North until 6 P.M. They wait in their cars or on benches outside.] What, they're counting everybody? How do you know that you can't take $20 bills in there or $10 bills, that it has to be fives and ones? And there may be no food in there, so you better eat before you go in there. You don't know these things. I mean, when I first thought of visiting, I thought you visit in their cell. I thought you were escorted to their cell. I didn't know there was a big room to visit in. 'Cause what do you believe on TV? (Marie)

I think there should be more generalized information, what to expect when you get to the prison. You're going to have to stand in line, you're going to have to do this, you're going to have to do that. There's no information like that put out at all, as far as I know. Most people, when they come to a prison like this, they've been at another prison before for processing or coming from a county jail, most people figure they're already approved because they had visited before, and that's not the case. You might drive hundreds of miles, which happened to us. We were told by his counselor that he could have a visit because it was a holiday, and we got up here after traveling 420 miles, and they would only let us visit one day. And they weren't even going to let us visit that day, but we pleaded and cried. But I understand there's other people they've turned away. That's something that I think could be corrected. And when they transfer somebody, they could immediately notify their relatives as to where they're at, exactly when they can visit, what to expect when they do get there, what they should bring, what they shouldn't bring. . . . You have someone who has a couple of small children, a baby using diapers, there's restrictions on that. They can only bring so many diapers, and food can't be opened. There's all kinds of restrictions here that if they were informed ahead of time, it would cause less heartache and hardship on the family. (Betty)

COPING WITH VISITING STRESS

For some women, the visits are not negative experiences. In spite of the noise and lack of privacy, for some couples, the time is similar to a renewed courtship (Fishman, 1990; Holt & Miller, 1972). This may be a time of simply holding hands, better communication than before, a new degree of closeness, wearing their best clothes, and planning for the future. They learn to cope with the travel, the processing, the crowding of the visiting room, the attitudes of the guards. A primary coping mechanism is to stay focused on the purpose of visiting—to reunite the family—and to block out as much of the surroundings as possible. Some women close themselves off, becoming "emotional robots" (Koenig, 1985).

When I hit the visiting area before they completely check in, the first thing I do is pray that J___ is all right and that no unforeseen incident has occurred that would mess up our visit. Once I'm cleared from there, once I hit the visiting area, I forget that I'm visiting a prison and block out the surroundings, the guards, prison clothes, etc. My attention is only focused on the reuniting of our minds. It's a great feeling, and after the visit it's like I take on new strength even though I'm never sure of the exact date when I will visit again. (Charlene)

Well, I'm beaming because I'm with my husband. When I first started going there, I felt very depressed, worried all the time, showing my emotions when I left by crying. He would go back really sad and down, so I managed to curb that. But, as far as now compared to when I was first visiting, I have kind of, like, it's our own world, there's nobody else present. It's just you and I, and that type of thing, and that's made it a lot better. Plus, I have met a lot of people in there that are acting just like you were out on the streets, just talking, joking around, and you need that. They need it as well as we do. So as far as the visiting room itself now, it's not as depressing anymore. I say I'm going to see my husband, and that's my main purpose. (Terri)

When I get off the bus, I got butterflies in my stomach because I know I'm going to see him. I've learned to adjust to getting up at 3–4 o'clock in the morning, catching that early bus, taking that ride, the works. It's a three-hour bus ride getting here. 'Cause I know once I get there, I won't even think about the bus ride. All I'll know is that I'll be there with him. . . . I've learned to adjust to getting up there, getting in there, giving them my ID, my number, and sitting there and waiting. Sometimes I get a little frustrated when I get to the inside of those gates and he hasn't come out within 15 minutes or a half an hour. The guards, some of them are pretty cool. Some of them can get on your last nerve. They make things rough for you. "You're visiting a criminal, so I'm going to treat you like a criminal." Which is totally unfair. They don't have to do some of the things that they do. They don't have to act the way they act. They don't have to talk to me the way they talk to me sometimes. (Janet)

FRIENDS OUTSIDE

Another great source of support is Friends Outside. The Hospitality House in Salinas provides an inexpensive place to stay, facilities for cooking, and transportation to and from the prison for a minimal fee. As one wife said:

Friends Outside is truly a blessing to all who are loved ones of prisoners. They are friends that are needed and there in times of distress. They're great! (Charlene)

However, they do have rules regarding the hours they are open and the services they provide. At times, those rules conflict with the assistance the women need. Then they have to deal with their problems themselves.

I got stranded out there before. I missed the bus. . . . The only thing I can do is go and call Friends Outside and ask her can I come over and sit. And the attitude of the lady was, "No, you can't come over here and sit." I don't know anybody in Salinas. And the Friends Outside house is supposed to help you. She said, "Well, I can't help you with your problem. We're closed right now." I just hung up. I called a taxi and went to a 24-hour restaurant, that's the only thing I could think of. And I sat there until 3 o'clock in the morning, because the bus station was closing and the next bus going to O___ was at 3:20 in the morning. (Tijuan)

[After visiting and getting in a car accident on the way home outside of Gilroy] I called Friends Outside. And this girl that's staying there for the weekend answered the phone. I told her we were going to be coming there, could she go and try to wake M___ up, the lady who runs the house. Could you wake her up and ask her could we stay there? So, she couldn't wake her up. She says, "You guys come anyway." I say, "Are you going to stay awake and let us in?" She said, "Sure." So we got there, and the girl finally gets up and there's a bolt lock on the door, and she can't open it. We say, "Go get M___." She keep calling her and calling her, and we even went to a phone booth and tried to call her on the phone to see if we can wake her up to let us in. Finally, about 1:30, she answered the phone. I explained to her I was in an accident, we got kids, we're all wet, we have no money. Could we stay there until the next bus going back home? She said, "Well, I'm sorry, I don't know what I can do. You don't have enough money." Now, I've been there too many times and paid my $10 and donated money and everything. We just couldn't believe it. We had caught a cab from Hollister to Salinas, and the cab guy was nice enough to wait for us to try and see if we were going to be able to get in or what. So he ended up taking us to the bus station. It was closed, we couldn't get in. People standing outside, freezing. So he said, "There's a little café, you guys can wait here until the next bus going out." And finally about 4:15 that morning the bus came in. (Wanda)

Chapter 7

Dealing with the System

When he was in Central, he started college when he first got there. He went before the Board after he'd been there six months, and they really discouraged him. It was funny. Part-time work is very hard to find in there, and so he figured he had to get into something. His counselor said, "I will help you find a job." And they just have not found any work at this point. And when he went before the Board, they just really kind of discredited R___ and they said, "We don't understand this, you're living off the system. You're going to school." And I'm sitting there thinking, "Praise the Lord he's going to school, he is getting an education." Half those men wouldn't be in there if they had the proper education that they needed. So I was real discouraged. R___ said, "Sue, he acted like it wasn't good I was going to school, that I should get a job. Get a job painting or washing floors? How much education does that take? Anybody can do it. But I've never had an opportunity to really get a college degree and really learn something, get more educated. I'm going for it." He didn't let it discourage him. (Sue)

There are two officers who have talked to my attorney and are testifying on our behalf. It just blew my mind. And both of them offered. And that really surprised me. One of them overheard some of the harassment, some of the threats to R___. Plus he saw what they were doing to me in visiting. Some days I'd wait two to three hours [for them] to bring R___ out. It was a consistent thing, it wasn't one day, it was four days running. Every day they would harass me with my visits. I never once got up and complained. I never screamed and yelled. I didn't react the way they were programmed to believe that I should have acted. . . . And it's the same with R___. There's no doubt in his mind that on several occasions they pushed him for violent reactions, to the point where one officer undid R___'s handcuffs and said, "If you want to hit me, go ahead. This is me and you, off the record." R___ said, "Why would I want to hit you? I'm not a violent man." This angered the guy. He called R___ a pussy. R___ knows darn well he would have been in the hole for the rest of the duration. And he knew he was being pushed. See, this is their form of retaliation. This is their harassment. "I'll get him to go off on me." This is wrong. But you try to convince Joe Q. Public across the street that those things go on, it's impossible. (Misty)

[I worry] all the time. 'Cause I guess there is problems all the time: stabbings, beatings, taking advantage of each other. And there's all kinds of dope and everything else that goes on in a prison. It's probably worse than it is out on the streets. And as I said, F___'s a very timid-type person. I worry more about him than I would somebody else, 'cause he's the type somebody can push around, shove around, take advantage of. And emotionally, he had a nervous breakdown, so he's really a sick person in the wrong place. He shouldn't be in a place like that. When he was in County, he was seeing a psychiatrist on a regular basis, and they had him on antidepressants. But since he's been up here, he hasn't had any counseling at all, none at all. (Betty)

One of the hardest aspects of loving someone in prison is being powerless over the system's rules that govern the men's daily existence and the families' interactions with their loved ones. The interactions range from the frustrating to the brutal, but there is always an insecurity and underlying anxiety that something could go wrong.

For the men, it is a system of no privacy, paperwork that could inaccurately represent you, rulings that could go against you, rumors, mistrust of everyone, constant fear of physical attack, mind games, boredom, deprivation, and total lack of control.

For the women, there is the worry about their husbands' safety, unpleasant interaction with guards, endless waiting, possible car searches, threats of visit termination, worry about violating the inconsistent dress codes or the rules relating to packages and family visiting, and all the planning of transportation, lodging, and food. These issues take on great significance beyond interaction with the prison. The women are making plans for their families and their future related to jobs, housing, legal options, and so forth. These concerns make evaluating their choices very difficult, and the women feel they are subject to extreme control by the Department of Corrections with its bureaucratic inconsistencies and general lack of information (Koenig, 1985). This is similar to the feelings of many low-income mothers who are dependent on the welfare department's power to deny or approve their benefit requests (Dill & Feld, 1982)

He was RTQed [restricted to quarters] for two days because there was some equipment missing from the paint shop, their grates they use for rollers for painting. In the chrono [report] that ends up in his file, the way it sounded when it was read was like he took them. "Forty-four pieces of iron that could be filed down into weapons out in the yard somewhere." So he has to write a 602 [a grievance filed by a prisoner] to pull that from his chrono. . . . Now they've got all this paperwork, and if the inmates aren't aware of it, it will stay in their chrono. . . . All those things look bad. They emphasize the bad and really try to diminish the good. It's a defeating situation. The inmates that are not aware that that exists and don't go out of their way to correct it will carry that forever. (Carrie)

The past few months have been horrible. Probably the most depressing time. It's scary. 'Cause he should have been out, and I cannot believe it. So, at this point right now, I know they can't keep him past next March, but it's such a desperate feeling that they're going to try something else to keep him here. . . . I don't even think about next week. I think about today. Because I can't. If I think about next Monday, the hearing should have been, the fact that tomorrow should be a hearing. If he doesn't have a hearing tomorrow, I couldn't handle it. So I don't think about it. It's the ninth Monday. For eight Mondays he was supposed to have had it. The first one he went to UCC, they're Unit Classifications. Then he couldn't go . . . the next Monday because the chrono wasn't there. It wasn't prepared yet. And the next Monday was a lockdown. And then the next Monday the chrono came out, but they had inadvertently left out a phrase, "referred to FCC" [Full Classification Committee]. So then he had to wait until the next Tuesday to go to UCC to get referred to FCC. And then the next Monday was a lockdown. And then the next Monday, we were doing interviews. [Interviews are conducted by the counselors when they question the men about the incident that caused the lockdown.]   (Colleen)

I wrote one letter one time to [Superintendent] S___ because I sent a package February first and he didn't get it until March fifth. So I wrote a letter, I wanted to know why. . . . The package is there; if everyone's on lockdown and they can take a guard to bring a person over for a visit, they can have the guard take him over to get his package. Granted, they are in there, I told Mr. S___, because he did wrong by the law. But at the same time, he's a human being and I said I had spent hard-earned money to get that package there. I felt it was only my right as a citizen that they shouldn't be holding up my mail. They said, "Procedures. When they're on lockdown, blah, blah, blah." And they said one time that he had gotten the ducat [pass to go somewhere or approval to purchase something] and because he was, they said, 15 minutes late [and they were closed]. . . . But they had closed the window two minutes early is exactly what happened. Of course, by the time the report got written up, he was 15 minutes late. So therefore he didn't get his package for a month. (Vicky)

PROCESSING

Frequently, incidents occur during processing, which all visitors must go through. This is where you are checked as an approved visitor for that prisoner—your identification is checked, your belongings are searched, your money is counted, and you walk through the metal detector. Visitors wait together as the processing occurs, perceiving the mood of the guards on duty.

Their dress codes and stuff, I think that they're so rigid about every little thing. I think they could bend a little bit, but then it depends on who's the staff at the time. 'Cause I've gone to visit at Soledad, and they weren't going to let my sister-in-law in one day because she had on this sleeveless top. It was sleeveless, that's all, and if you got all the way there and then they wouldn't let you visit? That's pretty evil. (Marilyn)

I had my hair rolled up on top of my head and the bobby pins kept setting [the metal detector] off. And she told me I had to take my hair down. I said, "I'm not taking my hair down." Well, I defied her is what it all boiled down to. And so she said, "Well, you'll have to be searched then." I said, "Well, you're just going to have to search me, then." Ever since then it's been nothing but hassles. . . . This one girl walked in, she might as well have had, as far as I'm concerned, just nylons on. And she walked in with that, no bra, you know. And I get turned away for wearing something that's just eyelety. And there's nothing seductive about it at all. I'd worn that top a million times before. . . . It's like I don't know where they draw the line. They're not consistent. (Cynthia)

Then [another] thing with them that I got angry about was when I had my chemotherapy. I started losing my hair slowly, and my hair was my pride and joy. And it was really hard on me, number one, to lose my hair, and it was hard on my vanity and my dignity. Well, I went out and bought a wig, and I had the rest of my hair shaved. The first day I showed up, they made me go into the strip room and take it off and they'd look under it. Well, most of them did it with dignity and class. I had one officer who every time she would get me, she'd take it upside down and shake it till it stuck out like Tina Turner. Then she'd hand it back to me and give me the little mirror that they look up vaginas with on the searches, hold it up in my face, which I did not want in my face, and expect me to be able to put it back on. Well, I got upset over it and I wrote a letter. They told me, "Too bad, too sad. We're protecting the security of our prison." So when I talked to K___ of the ACLU [American Civil Liberties Union], he told me to get a Baggie and fill it with dry chunk dog food, put it in the pocket of a skirt, and go in. I go to the prison and I have in my pocket a Baggie of dog food. I walk through the processor, they take me in the room and search me, they check my wig, there's nothing under my wig. Machine did not go off. I go over there where the counter is for visiting. The Sergeant was sitting there, and I reached in my pocket and I put the Baggie of dog food on the counter, and I said, "This is dog food; it could have been pot. It's not under my hair, it was in my pocket. I would not shave my hair off to be able to smuggle drugs. I would either put them in my pocket or put them up my keester like everybody else does. I'm just trying to make a point." And everyone stopped searching me except for the one woman who continued to harass me. (Misty)

CAR SEARCHES

One of the more insulting procedures for visitors is going through a car search. They are unannounced; when you drive onto the prison grounds, the normal route is blocked, so they cannot be avoided. Visitors feel the assumption that they are carrying contraband is insulting. It is that guilt by association that plagues the families of prisoners. Car searches take a long time, usually hours, cutting into precious visiting hours. During a car search, everything is removed from your car, guards search all the compartments of your car and under seats, while dogs jump in every area to sniff for drugs. The phones for the men are cut off, so they are not able to warn their visitors of the impending search. While there are some people arrested for carrying drugs or what are considered to be concealed weapons, often innocent people (primarily passengers) also lose their visits. Some experiences are quoted here at length.

We had stayed over Saturday and I was going to . . . visit Sunday morning. So, we got a room over in the city of Soledad, at the Hacienda Inn. The evening before, I had made arrangements with Friends Outside to pick us up over there at the Inn. So that morning they never showed up. I was wondering how come they didn't come and get us. It just so happened that another lady that was staying in the hotel was going to visit. She volunteered, "Do you guys want to ride with me?" I said yeah, I was glad. I wanted to be there. So we all got in the car, it was me and two other ladies. As a matter of fact, Janet was with me, she had her son, and this other lady, Jackie. Anyway, we gets in the car and this lady has her little boy with her, too. We gets in there, and we find out they're searching. I see the Friends Outside van, so this is why they didn't come and get us. We drive on up in there and we said, "Is everybody clean, you got anything? Get rid of it if you do." So everybody sitting up calm and cool. I guess everybody knew they was clean, so they didn't think about it. The girl, too, she said, "Well, I ain't got nothing." All of a sudden they tell us to pull in, past these other cars, instead of having them in line [and] having them go accordingly. They had us pull on in, real quick. They had us get out and everything. It just so happens this girl lives in S___, and she comes back and forth all the time by herself and her baby. So she had a billy club, but it had a chain on it in the middle and two sticks on the side. Some type of weapon. They considered it being a concealed weapon. She had it under her seat. They asked her, "Well, who does this belong to, Ma'am?" She said it was one of her friends. She said he just happened to have left it in her car. She kept it there as protection for her in case something happens when she's traveling. And they took her, took her baby. They went through all our things and everything. They didn't find anything. But they denied our visit, we couldn't visit for that day. Talk about being mad. They wouldn't even let us walk off the grounds. They took us in one of those police cars and just drove us onto the road. We waited there for the Greyhound bus. They didn't consider letting us go back to make a phone call to have someone come and get us or something like that. I couldn't believe that because she had something in her car, and we didn't have nothing to do with that, it was just something she had done and it was in her car. So they denied our visit. That was my first time having an experience with them. That was a bad experience. (Wanda)

My first complaint was with the car searches. I got arrested for having two birth control pills in my car, which the officer that arrested me swore to God that these were heavy-duty narcotics. These were "cross tops," I think he called them. They slipped up with the charge. They were supposed to charge me with possession of narcotics, and they charged me with possession of narcotics with intent to smuggle. Now if you read the penal code number, it means that they found them on your body. They found them under the passenger seat of my car. And they were extremely dirty. They were even noted on the arrest report, "dirty white pills." I lost my visits for 13 days. And the laboratory report came back, "not a controlled substance." I didn't yell, I didn't scream. I spent 28 hours in jail with the meanest women I have ever met in my entire life. They just did not like me. I had a very difficult time surviving. It was Monterey County Jail. I was placed in with already convicted felons. The girl underneath me was in for murder. She was ready for transfer to CIW [California Institution for Women]. Now I'm told that's against the law. Well, this girl did not like me at all. I had a very hard time. Probably another six hours, and I would have been either extremely beat up or dead, 'cause they were out to get me. I just did not fit in there. And when I ran out of cigarettes, I couldn't go to the bathroom, 'cause every time I had to go to the bathroom, they'd make me give them two cigarettes. If I used the phone, it would cost me two cigarettes. Thank God I had two packs of cigarettes and I only stayed 28 hours. It was bad. I got one apology from anyone at the prison. . . . I was told by the ACLU that I could file for false arrest, and I chose not to— don't buck, they're doing a job. They made a stupid screwup. (Misty)

I happened to get caught in the car search. No biggie, I wasn't really worried about it. But I had this girl staying here with me at the time, and she was going on a family visit. So we get in the car, I take her down to the grocery store and buy her food. She comes out and we're loading up the car, and there is this Mexican girl standing up against the wall with a little boy. She says, "If I give you $3 for gas, can you take me to the prison? I've got a family visit." We took her in the car, we got down there and saw there was a car search. I didn't care, I wasn't worried about it. . . . Then they went through my car, through all the grocery bags. I seen the dogs go into my car and out of my car and they didn't find nothing. About 15 or 20 minutes later, this [guard] comes out with a piece of grass. I mean, it wasn't even as big as that pinhole. He says, "We found this in your car." I says, "What is it?" He says, "It's marijuana." I say, "It ain't no marijuana, it's lawn grass." He says, "No, it isn't, it's marijuana." I says, "Why don't you have it tested?" He goes, "In order to see your husbands, you have to go through strip searches." I say, "Hey, check that out before you accuse me, there ain't no marijuana in my car." I was getting mad. They take it in and I knew it wasn't marijuana. They come out and tell me it was marijuana. So I say, "OK, go ahead," and I go through the strip search and everything. It didn't take me and S___ long to go through it, because we didn't have nothing. This girl we picked up at the store had cocaine on her. And they come out and get me. They say, "Are you Catherine H___?" "Yes." "Will you follow us please?" I says, "Real good, the damn broad had something on her." I got in there and they read me my rights. They didn't have to do that to try to scare me. There was a lieutenant in there and one of those CDC [California Department of Corrections] plainclothes guys. I go in there and he goes, "How long have you known this lady?" I said, "Altogether, about two and a half hours." "What do you mean two and a half hours?" I says, "I picked her up at the store before I came here. She asked me for a ride and offered me $3 for gas to take her to family visiting. That's why she's here." The other guy goes, "She told us she knew you." I go, "If she knows me, she knows me from seeing me right there at the prison. Other than that, she don't know me." He goes, "Well, she said she calls you all the time." I says, "You go out there and ask her what my phone number is. What are you trying to say? I don't know her, I gave her a ride from the store, and if you go out there and bring her in and ask her in front of me if she knows me, she'll tell you the truth." Then he goes, "Well, are you in the habit of picking up strange women in places up at the stores?" I says, "Yes, when they need a ride to over here, especially when they offer me gas money. Even if she didn't offer me gas money, I would probably have picked her up." "Well, there's no reason to get smart." I go, "I'm not getting smart, I'm telling you the truth." "Well, she was found with cocaine on her and she says she knows you." I said, "Well, she can continue to say she knows me until her face is broke. But I am not going to cop to knowing her when I don't know her. Do you think I'd let a friend stand out there without copping to knowing them?" He didn't say nothing. He then tried to tell me if I don't watch my step they are going to arrest me, etc., etc. . . . So we lost our visits. (Cathy)

HARASSMENT

Whether the wife or the husband is harassed, it affects them both. Loss of the privilege of visiting time is a common outcome. Pat searches or strip searches and extra watching are other forms of harassment. The prison maintains that these actions are needed for security. The families see them as harassment to discourage the family bond and as retaliation against prisoners for having broken the law in the first place.

He was moved due to a cell change, took his boxes in, left them, they were going to the yard. Came back and they had found a weapon in their cell. Both the cellie [cellmate] and my husband knew nothing about this weapon. And T___, who was my husband's cellie, says, "Is it yours?" "No, is it yours?" And he's going, "No, but hey, I'll cop to it. It's my cell, you just moved in." And so T___ says, "It's mine," and the officer says [to my husband], "That's a more serious 115 [a disciplinary rules violation report], you're threatening his life if he doesn't ride the beef for you." So, with this, he goes to the hole, and in the hole we appeal all the way to Sacramento. And I was fighting for his side of it, and the program administrator said to me, "Frankly, Mrs. D___, if I have my way, whatever it takes, I'm keeping him in the hole till his maximum date out. He'll never be out of the hole." I said, "Did I hear you right?" He said, "You heard right. If I have to plant something on him, he'll stay in the hole. And there's frankly nothing you can do about it." "Watch me." I was hot! That's why I'm very disgusted. I got him out of the hole. They kept him in for two months longer, but I got him out. . . . But they did plant stuff on him in there. They played all kinds of games. After he got out, just a couple of weeks ago, he got a thing from the counselor, he got a 115 for manufacturing alcoholic beverages in the hole! How can you manufacture alcoholic beverages in the hole, where he's given his morning little bowl of cereal? There's no way. (Colleen)

Another incident occurred in June of 1986, when my husband was falsely charged with a serious offense because of exercising his right to file 602s on overexaggerated 115s by this sergeant. On going to receive a grant or denial on one of these 115s during a lockdown of blacks, only disrespectful remarks were made from the lieutenants and sergeants to my husband, which triggered my husband to make one to them. All this is taking place during the hearing or appeal. This evidently upset the officers and led to racial slurs like, "You think you're tough, nigger," along with a push and shove from the officer, which wasn't called for. After that a number of COs, sergeants and lieutenants, came, used excessive force to handcuff J___. After J___ was handcuffed, one sergeant squeezed his testicles while another choked him and charged him with assault. The hearing on this incident was extended and extended. Our life and relationship and privilege was in an uproar. After writing many letters to the superintendent, program administrator, D. M___, law firms, state assemblypersons of state and Salinas, and others, exposing their abuse of power, conspiracy, and wicked works, the tables turned. The truth started becoming manifest, and even though J___ was found guilty of assault charges, the incident report that was written up never stated an actual assault or attempted assault. There was never any evidence to support guilty findings, and after two and a half months, one of the program administrators had the nerve to ask my husband how did they find him guilty? We all know that these false charges were their way of retaliating and making inmates and families suffer. This was a very painful and stressful and frustrating situation that me, my husband, and daughter have experienced. To top that, this is August and the summer is just about over and our prospect of spending one summer day together as a family is about over. During this accusation, my husband lost his job, one of the better ones, and his prospect of moving up as a lead man; we lost our family visits, one of which we would have had this summer; we lost communication over the phones, regular contact visits, had to visit behind glass, and he lost his Full Committee meeting to get points lowered and be moved from maximum to medium custody, which means he could be transferred closer to home. So I'm sure they accomplished their purpose. (Charlene)

When this started happening with my husband, no matter what number I had picked to come in, they always made me the last person, and I had to sit out in the foyer until after J___ came in. They would strip search him on the way in, and either tell me they wanted to strip search me or they patted me down more times for no reason. For a while the metal detector would seriously break on the two people before me every time when I went in. I thought that was a little off. . . . The local people are watched twice as much as anyone else. I think that's part of the problem, is being local. The fact that now three of the local people are in O-wing, well, I can't speak for the other people, I can only speak for myself, I never took drugs in. And they watch you. I've been in the visiting room when there's a couple over next to the [vending] machine being very crude, yet the guards didn't notice them, but at the same time their eyes were glued to myself and my husband and about three other couples who are regulars. (Cyndi)

LAWYERS

Negative experience with the system very likely began before the husband's arrival at prison. Most people who end up in prison are poor—they couldn't afford a good lawyer. In many cases, a court-appointed public defender is so overworked, he or she may not have the time to properly handle the case. Some lawyers don't even meet with their clients. There is the feeling that the defendant is a pawn in someone else's game, in which the sentencing rules and procedures are arbitrary and impenetrable by the lower social classes.

Swan (1981) similarly found that wives were not given adequate information by lawyers to make informed decisions on how to use their limited resources. Lawyers frequently did not explain the consequences of certain decisions, the chance of acquittal, or the possible sentence length. They were too often inaccessible and had negative attitudes toward their clients. Furthermore, in his study of families of black prisoners, Swan felt that the criminal justice system was one more part of the pattern of control and domination of the black community.

I just think it's pretty terrible for people who don't have any money. They have to depend on a public defender. And either you have a good one or you don't, and you never really know. If you had $120-200,000, he might not be here right now, you know. So, as far as that goes, I don't have much faith in our public defense system, courts, any of it. Even through my own personal experience with divorce and child custody and all that, I have no faith in the court system whatsoever. Which is why he plea-bargained. He figured he'd get a better deal that way than if he went through the whole thing. (Betty)

My experience with lawyers during J___'s trial was a very negative experience. His public defender played judge and jury and found him guilty before his preliminary or jury trial ever started. I feel my husband was railroaded in one way or another. (Charlene)

I paid for a lawyer. He never talked to my husband. At the last minute, my husband said, "No, I'm not taking that time. I paid you all this money and you never came and talked to me. Now you're telling me to take nine years. That's the best you could do? Hell, no!" And he told him that in front of the judge. The lawyer got pissed. I was walking, he caught up to me, "He can rot in hell for all I care." He was a well-known lawyer in S___, the best. He walked out on my husband. He told me, "He embarrassed me in there. He can rot in hell for all I care." Like his neck was on the line. So my husband didn't take it. He sent a representative, one of his workers, to take the case. I wrote a letter to the judge to forgive my husband, that he has changed, that I was something new in his life. The judge went down two years on him and a year served. So from nine to seven. But it didn't help with the lawyer that I paid all that hard-working money. (Minerva)

WORRIES

The women know that life inside the prison is dangerous and stressful. They try to stay optimistic, but they can't escape the worry that something out of their control will happen to their husbands in there. There is worry about their physical and mental health, and worries about gangs. There is the fear that maybe they won't make it out alive. This fear of safe return is shared by families of military men. Children and wives of seamen, for instance, worry about ships colliding and the crew drowning (Rosenfeld et al., 1973).

He don't really tell me everything that go on in there. He try to, but he said I probably wouldn't understand it. The different races together, and the gang-banging, and you have to be aware at all times. Sometimes you have to sleep with one eye open. Things like that worries me for him to have to tell me that. I want to know, like, is he okay. . . . [I worry] about the different gangs. I know while you're in prison you have to be in some kind of gang for protection. That's what I was told. For protection. You can't just be by yourself. You have to have someone. I'm very scared for him because he say the people ask you to be in their gang. You don't want to tell them no. They may all break out in a fight. So he's in one of them. And I'm really scared for him. I worry myself almost to death about a week ago. He was telling me they asked him to be in this other gang, and he told them no. Then I'm thinking, what are you going to do now, are they going to hurt him, are they going to set him up? (Sharon)

I never know if he's going to walk out of there alive. You don't know. And this is every day. And I think, there's times when I've gotten down and depressed. I try not to think about it, but there's times when I've just broken down and cried. . . . I think it had been a couple of days I didn't get a letter and I was getting panic-stricken. I'm ready to walk out and get into that Jeep and drive up here to make sure he's okay, because you don't know and don't trust the system. I don't trust them as far as that goes. I think that's probably the main worry, that you don't know if they're going to walk out of there alive or not. And the longer the time that they have, the more that you have to worry about it. And it bothers me. I think I had mentioned it to a friend that they take life like a joke, and I said, "You can sit there and joke, I'll joke with you about different things. That's okay because I have a great sense of humor. At least I think I do. But let's not forget one thing. We don't know if they're going to come out of there alive." And to be honest about it, I don't know what I would do if he didn't come home. (JoAnna)

He's not prejudiced in the least, and evidently you don't talk to the blacks, you don't talk to the Mexicans, if you are Caucasian. And that's really hard for him to deal with because a lot of his friends are black, in there or before, too. Because he doesn't judge people, and it's based on the relationship, period, not by how they treat other people, but his relationship, period. At first it was really scary because he was having warnings from the gang leaders of the white groups, saying, "Hey, listen, you're talking to that nigger," as they would say, "and we don't like it." P___ said, "He's a human being, and I'll talk to whoever I damn well please." And he said at first he found himself being intimidated by that, not being with somebody because they were black or Mexican. He said the guilt was just too much. . . . It's hard for us both to deal with, the prejudiceness. And that still is my fear, that somebody's gonna get pissed that he's talking to somebody they don't like, and stick him for it. That's really depressing. Same with him. I think that's one of his biggest fears, is someone getting mad because he's associating with somebody he cares for, as a friend, as a person. (Marie)

The women are also greatly concerned about the health care of prisoners, the environment, and what will happen upon release. Women in Koenig's 1985 study indicated two main concerns about their husbands—their safety and how imprisonment would affect their personality and behavior upon release.

I worry about his health because his health is bad. He's got ulcers from being in there 'cause there's an awful lot of things to worry about. Sometimes I worry, but everybody just tells me that he's going to be okay, and that I don't have to worry so. I know he knows the system, he's been in there for too long to fool with anything that could hurt him. He knows the wires in there, so he thinks it would be unnecessary to worry. When they're locked down, I worry about his mental well-being. Mostly I worry about him being able to do the time and not be bitter. I worry about that. I'd hate for him to come out and be so bitter that he couldn't be happy. (Marilyn)

He has a recurring ear infection, and he's gone to the doctor before about it and they give him antibiotics. So it goes away, and after the antibiotics are gone, it will come back. And I know there's got to be something they can do. People on the outside don't live with ear infections. They get over it. But in order to go to the doctor in there, they have to go and stand outside at 7 o'clock in the morning until 8 o'clock in the morning. And it's windy out there and it's cold, and if they're very sick, they just get sicker. So my husband, unless he's dying, he would rather go to work and just bear with it rather than stand out there and get even sicker. I do worry about him being in there because you never know what can happen. He could be in the wrong place at the wrong time. One guy was talking on the phone to his mother and got his knee shot because the guard [shot into the yard at some Mexicans and the bullet ricocheted]. (Laura)

My primary concern about my husband's release in society is that whatever trade or trades he comes out here with or whatever job he qualifies for, that he will be given equal opportunity and not be discriminated against because of being an ex-con. I believe that him having a stable and good-paying job will contribute to his success in society. (Charlene)

FAMILY VISITING PROBLEMS

Family visiting is another major area of complaint, relating mostly to the number of days available for visiting and the frequency of visiting. But there are some other problems. Cockroaches, broken furniture, heaters or ovens that don't work, or even having a visit canceled due to bureaucratic mix-up are not uncommon. Mix-ups related to scheduling were also cited by women in Bloom and Cohen's study (1981).

The trailers and apartments are nice, but I don't think that there should be these roaches and all that around. There's no excuse for that. That puts a damper on your visit, for one thing. Another thing with family visiting is the fact that you go and you drop off your things in the morning and they wait until you get there at 12:30 or 1:00 before they start going through them, and you don't get in there until 3:30-4:00. So there's half of your first day already gone. And they don't really care. And I don't feel there's any reason for that. They've had all that time to go through and search your things, so all you would have to do when you got there was to be processed through and taken onto the van. I think that that's wrong, especially when you wait so many days for your visit, and half of your first day is already gone. You only have the next day to be together. That depresses me. They should have at least two days, like they say. And they could very easily make that possible. (Terri)

Mrs. Y____ called me up that day and asked me, "Sue, can you come down?" It was on a Tuesday, and it was for that Friday. And I said, "Yeah, but . . ." and I was telling her the story of what was happening, that I would get off work at three and drive, and I wasn't sure if I could make it, but I accept and I'll try to make it. I get down there, they didn't have me scheduled. They scheduled another girl. What happened is a trailer was open, but it had no television. And I said, "I don't watch much TV anyway, no biggie." R___ was the one who enjoys television, but I thought for him to get a visit, he'll sacrifice a television. So we got in. But they almost sent me home. (Sue)

It was our first family visit, and I was so excited. I had had my bags packed for a month. As soon as I'd gotten the application approved, I was ready. Everything was ready. So she called me and said, "Well, you can come on in. Be here by seven." "I'll be there by six." "No, just be here by seven." "I will be there by six." I go out, and in ten minutes time I had already called my company, had them sign me out on leave, everybody knew that I was waiting for my family visit. It was such a big, important thing to me, and they all knew. Ten minutes later there was a phone call, and my friend came up just looking really down. "Jeni, it's Officer Y___ again, she wants to talk to you." I picked up the phone and she says, "I'm sorry, we've made a mistake. It's for protective custody housing unit. Your husband's in the wrong custody level, you can't have a visit." Well, in ten minutes, I went from—and I was eight months pregnant—ecstatic, I was so happy, to I just burst into tears. My friends didn't know what to do 'cause I was just so upset. Things like that can really ruin you. Plus they had already called W___ and told him to get ready for a visit. Apparently he was ready to pull out the sink and the toilet and throw things around! 'Cause we'd been waiting and waiting, I think it was 45 days or something like that. We were ready. And they pulled him, and then they called him back and told him that we couldn't visit. I got off work and I went straight over there. . . . I had to, because I needed his strength. I was so torn up. (Jeni)

Family visiting is an enormous part of the family effort to maintain any sense of normalcy. The other conceivable ways are either not explored by the prison or are rarely done. Family activities within the visiting room are rare. Families have some ideas that they believe are reasonable, but prison officials have not been receptive. Visitors view the lack of attention to families as a reflection of the system's insensitivity.

The kids [should be able] to bring their homework in. That's really unfair. Normally you have your parents help you with your homework. They can't, because they're saying, "No, you can't bring it in." It's a family situation. Anything that revolves around a real family situation they try to suppress. (Carrie)

There is absolutely nothing in the visiting room to make a family feel comfortable. They offer no special programming for inmates there with their children or their families. They could make the room look more pleasant and not like a prison, to make people feel more comfortable. Their theory is Friends Outside, but it's outside, comes in the prison and takes your kids away. [The children are] there to visit, they're there to be a family, but they [Friends Outside] come and take them away someplace where they can go and have fun and then come back. I think they could do something to organize more of a family-type thing. I don't know why they don't from time to time have a little barbeque out there. For the amount of money people put in the machines, the wives would be very happy to contribute towards the barbeque. As long as the inmates are all confined in one room, where are they gonna go? They do have their Christmas party. . . . We went in and visited early and then the kids left when the party started. They didn't want to see their dad like that. It wasn't a joyous occasion. They're a little older, it's basically designed for smaller kids. But during the party, the inmates were allowed to get up and walk around. . . . It was a family thing. People are up eating cookies and having a good time. I don't see what it would hurt to do that more often. Why can't they do those things like at Easter . . . on different occasions throughout the year? (Misty)

I feel it would be great to have a counselor or meetings there at the prison with the wives and the family members to just have a big rap session. Discuss things that are going on. What do you do when you get out? Now, they do it with the men. I hear there's a prerelease program, and R___ sat in on one, one time. He said it was real neat. But I think throughout the whole time, there should be discussion involving the family. I agree that it should be for the men, but I feel that it would be great if they'd involve the family in it, too. So they could all sit around and talk. If they were to do that, to get a worker that would come in once a month and sit with a lot of families and discuss lifestyles and getting jobs and things like that, it would give them something to think about when they come home. I think it would be very healthy. It would give the man a real support, too, to sit with a family member and discuss these things and hear it come out of their mouth. But, I think that would take a real act of God to have that happen. 'Cause if they're not even dealing with the men that are in there now properly, why would they involve me and my children? (Sue)

Chapter 8

The Role of the Family

Family visits are important. I really think, from what I've heard statistically, family visiting and regular visiting hold a lot of bearing on whether they have return inmates or not. They're family support, they're holding the family together. This institution, I think, in a lot of ways pulls families apart. The whole system has a tendency to pull families apart more than what they are really supposed to do. Our family visits are good. We have a lot of fun, the kids enjoy it. They get to play like it's home....Her relating to having daddy around again was really funny the first family visit. 'Cause the kids went, "Well, dad's here. He's a male, it's a different situation here, mom." (Carrie)

For the kids' sake, [there should be] more activities for the kids with their fathers and mothers. They have this maybe once a year. Like the Christmas thing over there. It was nice, but they should have more programs. Kids' family day with their families. Different little holidays, because the kids miss out on the picnicking with the father and the mother and different trips. They need that support, so that when they grow up and have families, they will be strong, have a together family. They know only what we teach them. [Whether] their father's in jail or not, they need this family togetherness. (Minerva)

[It would be good for families] to tour part of the prison. They could take the guys out. Just to see the cells that they're in, what exactly it is that they're living like, 'cause he's described things to me, but I still can't grasp exactly how small their cell is. And he says there's some good things about it in there, but I have yet to figure out what. (Cyndi)

The wives have strong feelings about rehabilitation. They have a vested interest in the day-to-day lives of their husbands as well as the long-term impact of the incarceration. After all, the women are experiencing the imprisonment along with the men. Universally, the women are disappointed and disheartened with the treatment of the men and how that treatment affects them. Most feel their men are paying for their crimes by virtue of the fact of being locked up and deprived of their freedom. But there are additional punishments prisoners suffer, and these run contrary to their rehabilitation and hope of being productive, positive citizens of society.

I have yet to see any rehabilitation actually being done. I talked to C. L___ with the Department of Corrections in Sacramento on rehabilitation. She states that the schools in there are rehabilitation, that their jobs are rehabilitation. So I told her, "You're going to tell me that you give a guy a job sweeping the floors for $12 a month and he's being rehabilitated? He's being used and abused, and he knows it, and he's not an idiot. He's slave labor. Prisons are big business." (Misty)

Why are they spending all this money for new prisons? Why don't they spend some of it on some type of rehabilitation? Why don't they spend it on programs so that when they go out, they've got something where they make good money, where they don't have to go rob places, they don't have to steal to survive? There's better ways they could spend the money, and I don't think building new prisons is it. (Jeni)

PSYCHOLOGICAL IMPACT

Wives frequently cite the harassments and threats that affect the men psychologically. The New York State Defenders Association writes in its report, *What Prisons Do to People* (1985, p. 5), that by depriving people of "relationships and activities that foster self-esteem, and forcing them to live in dehumanizing conditions, prison diminishes self-worth and intensifies an individual's sense of powerlessness." The wives are concerned about the men's low self-esteem and see prison as a place that tears men down and makes them bitter (Rollo & Adams, 1987).

To rehabilitate prisoners, I think that first of all, rather than throwing them in prison and treating them as animals, they should continue to treat them as humans. I think that the way that the prison system deals with them inside makes them more of a criminal when they come out. They also need more inside activities, jobs, and education to give them something to strive for and want to live for while they're in there. It's a lot of prisoners that go in straight but come out heroin addicts and dope fiends because there's nothing to strive for, so they resort to homosexuality, drugs, and violence to deal with prison life. Those prisoners need some type of ladder of success to climb and goals they can strive to reach which will give them a reason to want to live and change. (Charlene)

First of all, it's just a business to them. They don't even consider these are human beings. And that's exactly how they end up feeling. And when they come out, I think they're more detrimental, a lot of them, when they come out than when they went in there. 'Cause they're more down, they're bitter. . . . Everything's so negative, and they need to be taught the positive. They already have low esteem. They don't think anything of themselves. Almost all those crimes committed are drug-related. And why do people have to escape through drugs? 'Cause they don't feel like they're about anything. (Cynthia)

They should try and believe that the guys are going to straighten up instead of trying to prove to guys that they aren't. To me it seems like they are just trying to keep them corrupt and mad and hateful and ugly, so that they can keep them in there and make more money. They're trying to make the guys go off. The whole time that my husband was in the hole, they had these 115s on him, even the day we had our second contact visit, he thought that they were harassing us. It makes you so sensitive and so touchy to every little glimpse, every little thing they say or anything. You just want to slug them, it makes you want to go off. (Cathy)

If they had more facilities for the conjugal visits, take some of that property that they have near there, just make it one little village. Where more of them can have those visits at once, instead of just eight or nine. My God, just in one section alone there's like 2500 men. And cut down on the population in there. As T___ puts it, you walk around and someone steps on your ass half the day. You've got two men in a 6' by 9' cell. That's inhuman. . . . And the thing that the people there in that facility could do is quit instigating the fights. See, they want a constant dilemma between the blacks and Mexicans, the whites and the Mexicans, the whites and the blacks. As long as they don't cooperate with each other, they've got them. (Valerie)

COUNSELING

Employees of the prison who are called counselors are not counselors with degrees in psychology or training in social work. Rather, counselors in the prison system deal with paperwork. They handle all kinds of forms, requests, and so forth. Prisoners have to go through their counselors to get anything done, and counselors keep the files on the prisoners. The only therapists who may be in the system are at the medical facilities, such as the prison at Vacaville. Many wives are concerned that there is no counseling available. They feel there should be.

I think for any prisoner there should be psychological evaluation. There obviously is a problem or they wouldn't be in jail. And then, according to whatever came in their evaluation, they should be given counseling. I don't think they're getting that here. As far as I know, there is no counseling at all. He has a counselor, but that counselor strictly passes on good word or bad word. It's paperwork. There's nobody he can really go to . . . talk to if he's got a problem, other than his fellow inmates, which have problems themselves, so they're not exactly good guidance counselors at all. I think that's really a big downfall of the prison system. That's something that's definitely needed. And probably the biggest thing that they have working against them is that there's no counseling. 'Cause if you don't get to the root, I don't think it does a hell of a lot of good to put a person in jail and then not help them. This is supposed to be a correctional facility. (Betty)

It doesn't seem to have any kind of rehabilitation, period. The end. It's very simple.

You get in there, you get a job in there, painting, scrubbing the floors, whatever. That is not rehabilitation. And they're around a lot of men who tell you their game out on the street. They don't have men and counselors and psychiatrists coming in on a daily basis, meeting with men, men that have been into heavy drugs and say, "Let's discuss it, let's get back into your childhood," and sit around in a whole group of people and sit and discuss the problem. That's how I thought prison was, years ago. I had no idea that they just throw you in there and just say, "Make it, buddy, hope you make it out in ten years, five years, or whatever your sentence is. . . . " I think it should be mandatory for men to get in group meetings and really start getting some analyzing themselves, checking it out. "Hey, what got me in here?" Instead of sitting in their cell constantly thinking "Man, when I get out . . ." and having bitterness, which a lot of them do. (Sue)

PROGRAMS

Most women see the biggest problems as the lack of educational and training programs. Some programs do exist, but they are usually few, with waiting lists. Many programs have closed over the years due to budget cuts. Another problem has been that prisoners start a program and then are transferred, and thus are unable to complete the training. Jobs that are available are generally menial and low-paying, perhaps 15 cents an hour. Some men want to work, but the prison may not have enough jobs for everyone.

They're not doing anything now. What they do, is they have the public believing that they are. That is one of the things that just astounds me. They're putting this image out of all of the nice things and all of the different programs, but what they're not telling the public is how many things are closed down. They don't tell them about the overcrowding. It's starting to come out a little bit. They've got people in there that want to work, and they won't give them a job. People need to do something. They're getting bored, terribly bored. . . . They don't have anything for them to do, so they end up fighting over petty things. They end up doing things that they normally wouldn't do if they were on the outside. Because they're bored. They don't have the right kind of education. You've got a lot of people there who don't know how to read or write. (JoAnna)

I think [they should teach] these men, especially the men who are illiterate, how to obtain a job by just the small things of filling out a job application. There are a lot of people in there that don't even know that. Showing them how to dress, getting them career-oriented. More or less showing them how to react in society, to make it and stay out there. Not just open the gate, 'bye, you're gone, you do on your own whatever you do. Give them some learning techniques of what they're gonna expect from society, how people are gonna react towards them. (Terri)

I know a lot of guys who are working, taking a correspondence course through Hartnell, some of them, and they're going to school and getting their education. And then they're going on to get degrees. I think that they should continue that in more prisons, and they would find that the more serious ones would enroll in these and then be able to stay out once they get out. Just to walk out the door with $200 in your hands, what are you going to do, get an apartment for $200? Are you going to eat very long on $200? What if your family hates you, then what do you do? There's probably other programs and I don't know how those work, but I think that if they had a skill, then they would be better able to support themselves. (Laura)

Pre-release programs like work furloughs and halfway houses are available on a limited scale to eligible prisoners. The women feel these programs are very positive because they help to integrate the prisoner back into society at a slow rate. Many men leaving prison are put back into a very changed society. The fast pace, the demands, and the social interactions can be traumatic. Programs that ease a prisoner back into the mainstream help. Many wives in Koenig's study (1985) felt the men were out of touch with the realities of everyday life. The prisons do not allow the men to develop their life skills. The longer the prison term, the more likely that men become dependent on the system for their needs and lose subtle skills needed to make it on the outside (Irwin, 1980). In fact, as Rollo and Adams (1987) point out, prisoners live in a false world, and their families are essential in providing them with honest feedback about their future plans.

FAMILY ROLES

The couple will also have to readjust family roles, as the wife has most likely become very independent and established a new family lifestyle. Not all prisoners react positively to the control their wives have over their own lives (Hedin, 1986). The man has to fit into his family all over again, and initially may be as dependent on the wife on the outside as he was while incarcerated (Fishman, 1990; McCubbin & Dahl, 1976). Wives of military men similarly may develop a new maturity and self-confidence as they provide for their families. The family evolves without the presence of the husband/father, and there is a shift in family roles. This "closing ranks" may make reintegration more difficult (McCubbin & Dahl, 1976; Rosenfeld et al., 1973).

If they show they have straightened up, or show an improvement, they should be given less time or be given a little more freedom. They should be given more freedom a little bit at a time. As to it being black and white, like you're here now and then you're outside the gate, they should be allowed a little bit more freedom a little bit of the time to get them prepared. (Vicky)

If we had more halfway houses, I think that helps a lot of them. I have talked to quite a few friends that have husbands that have 10–20 years, it's like a new baby. They have to go out there and learn all over again. Things have changed. With a halfway house, they still have the security of the system, but they still have the freedom of going to work. And then they could, little by little, build up their confidence. It's hard for a person just to walk out in the clear blue open sky, no place to go, no job, a lot of them don't even have families, their wives have left them. So it's pretty rough. If we could have more community involvement to help. Just because a person made a mistake, you don't throw them away. There's more people out there doing wrong, they just got caught. There's more crooks out here than there is in prison. It's hard on the family. They don't know what to do when they get out. What is there for them to do? They got a record, what can they do? A lot of people don't want to trust them, they don't want to give them a chance. They need a chance. They need somebody to believe in them. To have an understanding, hey, give me a chance, I'll prove myself. (Jean)

THE FAMILY AS REHABILITATION AGENT

The family should be included as an active rehabilitation agent. Common sense tells us that feeling cared about and having a sense of belonging increases one's investment in behavior and its impact. The men have a greater stake in not committing crimes again to avoid the hardship that they have imposed on the family through this experience. Showalter and Jones (1980) point out that the love prisoners receive from their families enables them to see value in themselves; if they wait for their release, they have hope for the future.

The prison system needs to become pro-family, to support the family as a valuable resource (Swan, 1981). However, as Koenig (1985) points out, the corrections system does not encourage the wives in rehabilitative roles. While women try to figure out what is expected of them, they receive no credit from the system for all the time, money, and energy they invest in their incarcerated partners. Yet their involvement is clearly an important part of the rehabilitative process. Koenig states (1985, p. 114):

While the women believe that the role played by the Corrections System in their lives is unacceptable, it is fairly clear to them just what role is being played. The role played by the women in the management of the offender, however, seems to be unclear and the women struggle to establish a role that is acceptable to them and to the Corrections System.

Rehabilitation for him is being home, taking care of his family, making him feel like he's a man again. They took his freedom. He had to part with that. Spending more time with the family, making it better for the family. Getting the family closer, instead of harassing them, make them want to go visit. Sometimes I don't like to go on certain days because certain officers are there. Because I don't want to go through the hassles with the officer with their attitude. So I'm always finding who's on tonight? I know what type of attitude I should go in with or what personality changes I have to go through. Just getting us closer and making it easier for us. Especially for us out here. Fighting the system, fighting our husbands. They feel so guilty that they're not out here helping us, so we have conflicts. If they had more time with family, I think that would be big rehabilitation for them. (Minerva)

They need to cooperate with the families a little bit more. Just like when S___ asked to be closer to home, closer south, they moved him this far north. It's like they try to separate you, they don't work with you. And if they could work with you, if everybody worked together, we'd get a lot further. But they try to separate you. I don't know what their reasoning is, I haven't figured that out yet. [Maybe] it's 'cause they want to punish them, they want them to be totally without. But that isn't the answer. Nobody likes to feel like that. And I know if I were to feel like that, I wouldn't think too much of myself. I would think I was worthless. And I'd come out, "Well, I can't get a job, I'm worthless. Nobody's gonna want to hire me. I'm worthless." (Cynthia)

Many wives feel a strong obligation to help in the rehabilitation of their husbands. Their well-being is intimately connected to how well the men adjust to their release. They see their emotional support, encouragement, and trust as being essential to their husbands. The women hope to ease the adjustment to responsibilities, and they want to take the pressure off the men from feeling they immediately need to perform.

Fishman (1990) interviewed many wives who held traditional notions about marriage, feeling that the marriage must survive despite the husbands' lack of financial support or criminal acts they committed. These wives tend to deny the importance of the illegal behavior and feel overly responsible for the crimes their partners committed. They see their role in rehabilitation as fulfilling the role of wife. These wives sometimes put their lives on hold until their husbands returned.

The women in this study frequently talk of how they hope to have a certain level of material well-being by the time of release so the men can fit in, adjust, and then develop their place in society again. This kind of support is seen to be as important as the emotional support they give. In writing about black families, Swan (1981) comments that the families that are best able to survive as a unit are those in which the women deal realistically with the incarceration and are willing to struggle to keep the family afloat financially, sharing resources with the incarcerated partner.

I want to be able to have a place for him to go that he can call home and feel relaxed in. I'm getting money from this company I used to work with, and I want to put a couple of thousand aside so that he can get a vehicle when he gets out so things can fall into a certain cycle for him, that it won't be just coming out and having to start from the bottom. It's the way I feel like it's my duty to have things available or ready for him to come out into the world where he won't have to start at rock bottom. There will be something there to start with. (Vicky)

I think being behind the man totally, just being very encouraging, making sure that there are really good job prospects. That to me is probably one of the major things when he gets out that will keep him from not going back in, is getting a good job, earning a decent living. Because most men that are in there are in there because of greed, they wanted more, because the jobs that they had got were just so piddling that they weren't making good money, they couldn't totally provide for the family. That, to me, a job, is really important. A family, when they know that the man is getting out, that they really make some efforts in looking into a good job for him. And just being there to just totally love him and show him that they're going to make it. That he'll never go back again, because that prison's for animals, not people. (Sue)

The role of the family contributes to a great extent to the success of a parolee. It gives him a reason to want to live and want to change because of knowing someone loves, needs, cares, and depends on him being there. It gives him something to strive for and reach to, but most of all, maintain. Being J___'s wife, the closest one to him, I see my role as being a positive influence in his life when he is released. I realize that he may go through an adjustment period out here in society almost as long as he's been in the prison system. So being supportive, patient, and understanding will, without a doubt, contribute to his release. (Charlene)

SOCIETAL DOUBT

One of the more painful aspects of standing by and supporting someone in prison is the negativity and doubt of the society around you. While the wives feel the experience, though difficult, has meaning to it and can be turned into a strengthening experience, the people around them remain uninformed and misinformed about the prison system and the actual treatment of prisoners. Society is not inclined to see the human side of the prisoner—that is, unless and until someone they know and love gets incarcerated. The wives agree that going through the experience is the only way to truly understand and reassess views of prison and of punishment, of fairness and of rehabilitation. Negative media coverage of criminals and the political popularity of a tough-on-crime stance whip up a public sentiment devoid of compassion. That perspective is not only painful to the families, it's dysfunctional for the society, because then the society is not willing to support rehabilitation efforts that can truly help people turn around and become productive citizens.

I think the whole thing is that these people are human. The way the system is set up now, a prisoner is not only punished, the family is punished. Punished because they're separated, punished because they're so far away, punished because of the way they're treated by other people because their spouse or boyfriend or son, whoever it is, is in prison, and they're automatically put in another class. And that could probably be eased a lot. By just such things as the way they're treated, the way they're informed. That's probably the biggie right there, information. Treating people like they're human beings. They committed a crime, which anybody at any time in their life could do, depending on their state of mind, and they're still human beings and they should be treated as such. And I think that's probably what they forget. If it was one of their relatives, they wouldn't forget that. (Betty)

This one girl where I work said, "Well, you should just get rid of them so you don't have a problem anymore." I'm sitting there and I hear this, and I think, "I love this man. He's my husband. And you want to eliminate? Come on, what are you talking about?" And I don't think they really understand what they're saying. But they're not in that position, and they don't know the people that are there. (JoAnna)

People feel like, hey, a life for a life if a person's committed murder. They stole once, they'll steal again. It's an attitude that's been going on for years and years and years, probably centuries. I don't know if anybody could ever change that. Maybe they could make everybody go to a prison and spend one day, 'cause if you haven't been around it. . . . I was just horrified by what I've seen. The way they're treated. [And] you have an impression that prison isn't really too horrible from what you see on TV and hear, but the emotional stress and strain that it puts on the prisoner and his family is just terrible. There's no way to describe it unless you've been through it. I think the average person doesn't know what the prisons are. It's not the life of Reilly. And everybody thinks it is. (Betty)

Justice isn't fair. Prisons are full of poor people who couldn't afford lawyers, while there's a lot of crooks out there who are never going to be in prison because they've got money and they have good lawyers. My husband could probably be home now if we had enough money to get a good lawyer. And a good appeals lawyer wants about $6,000 to do his case. I talked to one in S____. If I had that kind of money, my husband would be home. I'm sure a lot of people get convicted for stuff they have not done, get time that's exorbitant because they couldn't afford a good lawyer. The whole system is corrupt, and besides being corrupt, people get arrested to make a quota, to put as many crimes as you can on one person because he cleans up the police sheets for unsolved cases. I don't think building more prisons will help. And it's expensive to build more prisons, expensive to maintain them. While I was staying at the hospitality house, I was reading some statistics. It said $100,000 to build one cell, that's how much steel it takes. And to maintain a medium-to-maximum-security inmate is $60,000 per year. And for a minimum it's $40,000. That's not money for their food. People read those statistics and they're not in the system, so they think it's because they're getting such good care. They don't know that really it's for guards. And if you ever go to these prisons . . . you see these guards make good money for very little work, and they're no mental giants. (Marilyn)

SOCIETAL COMPASSION

The women would like to see greater support for their role as wife of a prisoner who is trying to keep the family together and trying to help change and support her husband. If the public felt greater compassion, it would be a step forward in healing personal and social wounds.

Society has put on us a [guilt by association] if you're involved with a man in prison. . . . I used to think that, too, with my friend, and she was a good friend of mine. I was actually judging her. Now I look back, years back I used to think, "Oh, man, she has got a problem, a big one." And now I look at what I'm going through, and she looks at me sometimes and says, "Sue, do you see how it feels? Do you see what I went through?" And I used to say, "How did you make it? How did you do it?" She said, "I just did." And now I'm saying that, "I'm doing it." (Sue)

We feel like we're away from other people. We feel like they really don't know what's going on. So when you try to tell them, they just see the bad view. "It's a convict, I just can't see it." It's true they did the crime, but to help them, to get them off the streets, to really help them, they should try and have more people working in the system or showing they care. We could help the wives get strength and help the convicts out. If you don't help the wives, so the wives can help the husbands, we don't have no support. If anything, people down us for trying to help them. (Minerva)

The public does have a stake in the rehabilitation of prisoners. They do, after all, return to the outside society.

The reason that citizens should get involved in the prison is to see how it's run and what's going on inside, because everybody in there now is going to be out on the street. And if I could get involved, if I could volunteer time where I could go in and meet some inmates and talk to them and tell them about what's going on out here, make them feel like they're about something, tell them how good their artwork is, give them moral support, that's what they need. (Misty)

I worry about how he's going to be accepted. To me, him coming out into the streets, I would, to look at him, I would never figure he'd been a convict. Attitude and talk, and his attitude on life, it's just unbelievable. The closemindedness of people on the streets when they think about somebody being in prison. I guess I used to be the same way: they deserve it, blah, blah, blah. And when you get in and see the other side of it, it's not like that at all. I mean, granted, they did something wrong. They did have to be punished by the law, but at the same time they don't keep enough check on them to see if they've rehabilitated. (Vicky)

I think we can help change the public negative stereotype of inmates by helping to keep in front of them that we're all imperfect and we all make mistakes in our lives, but some greater than others. But that does not mean . . . we cannot be repentant, turn around, pay our dues to society, and abandon our former lifestyle and change for the betterment of ourselves and others. If they can show sympathy and mercy for a prostitute who abandons her life of prostitution, a drug abuser who abandons his life of drug abuse . . . then why not show the same sympathy and mercy for a criminal who is reformed and abandons a life of crime, especially if it's his first offense? (Charlene)

Try and reassure people that they have done their time. That doesn't mean that they're going to go right back out and do something wrong. That if they get together on the job, they're not going to be doing anything wrong, doing any stealing, doing any whatever you think you might not want to hire that person for. 'Cause that's what they went in there for, they have paid their dues. It's up to us to try to reassure them that they're going to be a better person than they was. If you were in that position, wouldn't you come out being a better person? So give the man a chance to prove himself that he can be one of the best employees you ever had. (Janet)

For a majority of people in society, their life is so fast-paced, nobody is thinking of anyone else but themselves and the almighty dollar. I think that . . . is what has caused a lot of these different crimes to be committed.   With more understanding, more closeness, more love, or just friendliness even, I think that society will turn around. (Terri)

Part III

CONCLUSION

Chapter 9

Prison Policy and Recommendations

The criminal justice system treats offenders as individuals rather than as family members with family roles, relationships, and obligations. We need to pay attention to the prisoner as the member of a family unit (Comiskey, 1989) and orient policy toward strengthening that unit. The prisoner's family, and his wife in particular, is in a unique position to provide community contact and moral support during incarceration, as well as help with release plans such as housing, employment, and money (Burstein, 1977; Morris, 1965). While the prison environment interferes with building and maintaining relationships (New York State Defenders Association, 1985), knowing that someone on the outside cares for him gives a prisoner some meaning to his life and a better chance of making it (Wylie, 1988).

Due to the husband's incarceration, the wife has to cope with myriad problems and stresses. The criminal justice system also ignores this impact on the family members when the offender is incarcerated. Wives find it difficult to lead normal lives as they deal with emotional loss, sometimes moving to remote areas where prisons are located but there are few jobs, facing financial hardships, feeling stigmatized due to their family ties with a prisoner, and trying to raise their children with one parent absent. The wives need assistance in dealing with the family reorganization (Carlson & Cervera, 1991; L. Smith, 1987).

Comiskey (1989) states that "vigorous efforts" should be made to keep families together, with every opportunity provided for family contact. We know that family contact helps lower recidivism rates and that prisoners have fewer disciplinary problems and stress within the prison when family contact is maintained. Koenig (1985) reminds us that the expectations of a family structure assist the prisoner in adjusting to life in the community. The family offers itself as an enormous resource base, and family-centered programs are not only cost-effective compared with reincarceration (Hairston, 1988a), but they are also humane. Family ties of adult offenders should be strengthened because this would result in safer communities and because the families of offenders are in crisis and deserve support (Family and Corrections Network, 1986).

RECOMMENDATIONS

The policy recommendations that follow are not new; they are those that address the views and suggestions of the women. Lawmakers need to take their voices into account. Repeatedly in this research, I have read statements or heard individuals say that the prison system disrupts families. Worse than a policy of benign neglect, the system seems to structure itself as anti-family. Visiting days and hours have been cut; visiting rooms are overcrowded, leading to early visit termination; family visiting is infrequent; there are no home furloughs (as of 1988 furloughs are possible in 48 states, the District of Columbia, and in the federal prison system, but not in California); family counseling is nonexistent; guards are rude and condescending; prisoners are located far from home; relationships with children and parents are disrupted; information is withheld from families; and harassment is common. Not surprisingly, the recommendations of service agencies and researchers address these issues in an attempt to restore family cohesion, lessen the stress and burden on the "free" family, and encourage the positive reintegration of the prisoner into the community.

Centerforce, a nonprofit organization established in 1975 to support prison visiting, reports yearly to the California legislature about its services and the barriers it perceives to prison visiting. Centerforce has visitor centers at 29 California prisons, and provides transportation, child care, emergency clothing, crisis intervention, information and referral, emergency food, and a rest spot before and after visiting. In fiscal year 1992–93, Centerforce's visitor centers provided 563,742 units of service to 236,890 prison visitors.

In its 1992–93 annual report, Centerforce described what it perceives as the eight major barriers for prison visitors. First, the transfer of prisoners from prison to prison creates enormous hardship on families who find it impossible to relocate due to cost and job considerations. The California Department of Corrections has the unenviable task of classifying and placing the flow of tens of thousands of prisoners in and out of the system. Centerforce recommends that this flow be reduced or stabilized by using more community-based resources instead of incarceration. These alternatives would lessen the burden on the prison system and allow us to address issues fundamental to crime and the community.

Second, arbitrary application of visiting room dress codes continues to create problems where visitors are turned away for lack of information about the rules, rules differing from one institution to another, or for inconsistent application of the rules by the visiting room guards. The solution Centerforce proposed in 1990—to have an 800 telephone number where callers could get the up-to-date information on rules and policies regarding visiting hours, dress codes, transportation resources, and so forth—was established in March 1993. With over 2,000 calls a month, this is a valuable resource. However, it does not address the arbitrary application of dress code rules by guards at the prisons.

Third, as the prisons themselves have become overcrowded, the visiting rooms are overcrowded. This results in early visit terminations. Centerforce recommends that visiting hours and days be increased. However, visiting hours have decreased due to budget cuts.

Reduced visiting hours constitute the fourth major barrier to visiting. Most California prisons were placed on a five-day visiting schedule in September 1991. Today most prisons have a four-day visiting schedule, and a few have two days (Saturday and Sunday). The present visiting schedule at Soledad is Thursday and Friday, 1:15 to 8:30 P.M. and Saturday and Sunday, 8:15 A.M. to 3 P.M. for general population prisoners. The hours are shorter for prisoners with noncontact visiting status (four days, shorter hours), those in administrative segregation (three days, shorter hours), and those on noncontact administrative segregation status (Sunday only from 12:30 to 2:30 P.M.). The rationale for these cuts was based on lack of money to pay for security (i.e., funding for visiting room guards). As prisons make their budgetary decisions, families are low on their list. In the eyes of the California Department of Corrections (CDC), visiting is secondary to their first priority, safety and security of the institution.

Fifth, Centerforce sees noncontact visiting as a problem. There are not enough telephones for the number of prisoners, and family contact suffers. More staff needs to be provided to allow either contact visiting or more telephones need to be installed.

Sixth, there is limited handicapped accessibility for visitors, especially in the older program sites. In order to fully assist visitors, Centerforce needs the funding to correct these problems.

Seventh, prisons are located in remote areas across the state, and families have difficulty getting transportation to visit. Centerforce recommends that public transportation be regionally coordinated so that buses and trains are available to meet the needs of the public that travel to prisons.

Last, insufficient funds for visitor programs is a major problem. While Centerforce serves a growing visitor population, child care and other supportive services have been eliminated or reduced. Yet services to visitors remain one of the most cost-effective services contracted out by the CDC. In Fiscal Year 1992/93, Centerforce provided services to 236,890 visitors, while experiencing a 5 percent budget reduction. These services include transportation, child care, information, clothing, and so forth, and Centerforce was able to reduce service cost to $5.21 per visitor. Continued program reductions don't make sense, given the nature of these programs—to maintain the family that supports the prisoner.

FINDINGS FROM RESEARCHERS

The most frequently cited recommendation related to prisoners and their families is to offer family counseling or workshops. These services could include wives and children, be throughout the prison system, and be provided by a private, nonprofit agency (Bloom & Cohen, 1981; Holt & Miller, 1972). Family counseling would allow the family to adjust to the impact of incarceration and explore the long-term effects (Fishman & Cassin, 1981; Schneller, 1976). Marital workshops might focus on communication skills, conflict resolution, community resources, relaxation techniques, and identification of needs for intensive therapy (Carlson & Cervera, 1991; Lowenstein, 1986; Swan, 1981).

Home furloughs, available in 48 states but not in California, also were frequently mentioned. Holt and Miller (1972) recommend that home leaves should be available to nonviolent offenders starting a few months after their imprisonment. These visits home would strengthen the family unit, enable the prisoner to carry out family roles, and allow the prisoner to continue contacts in the community. Home visits were also favored by Comiskey (1989), Fishman and Cassin (1981), Lowenstein (1986), and Schneller (1976).

Some researchers thought that family visits should be extended to common-law wives (Holt & Miller, 1972) or to any consenting adults (Bloom & Cohen, 1981). Prisoners who are not legally married have the same needs for intimacy and sexual gratification, and should not be denied this contact simply because they are not legally married. Family visiting is available in only 6 states (though most states have home furloughs, so conjugal visiting programs are not necessary), and there are many critics of the program. Program participants, however, see it as a major source of promoting the family by normalizing their lives and preparing them for reentry (Goetting, 1982b). Family visiting isn't an expensive program, given the benefits to participants. In 1992, there were 26,200 family visits in California at a cost of $120 per visit (Hart, 1993).

Providing more information in a coordinated fashion between agencies was mentioned by several reports (Bloom & Cohen, 1981; Fishman & Cassin, 1981), as was making transportation to the prisons available (Fishman & Cassin, 1981; Schneller, 1976). Providing more visiting opportunities and phone calls was mentioned by Fishman and Cassin (1981), Hairston (1988a), and Schneller (1976).

According to Hairston (1988b), policy needs to recognize visits between fathers and their children as a basic right. The few special programs that exist for children and parents are for incarcerated mothers; little attention has been paid to prisoners who are fathers. Special events such as picnics and parties can help normalize the reality of prison in the family's life. Hairston continues that fathers need parenting classes, and they need to learn skills to be able to work and provide for their children upon their release. Fishman and Cassin (1981) echoed the need for programs for children.

Barry (interview, June 12, 1991) claims that incarceration systematically destroys families when, due to lack of information and legal services, the children end up in foster care that leads to adoption. Parents are losing their parental rights in prisons all over the nation. Whether mother or father, the prisoner is worried about what is happening to his or her children but is unable to act on that concern. This is a monumental issue, requiring legislation to set up model programs to provide for family unification. In the long run, these programs prove to be not only humanitarian but also cost-effective.

Other recommendations include placing the prisoner closer to home (Holt & Miller, 1972), reducing restrictions and censoring of mail (Holt & Miller, 1972), liberalizing visiting rules (Lowenstein, 1986), lessening the punitive attitude of social service agencies (Lowenstein, 1986), providing guards with training to be sensitive to the needs of visitors (Hairston, 1988a; Mustin, 1988), providing more rehabilitation programs and self-help groups for prisoners (Lowenstein, 1986), improving visiting room conditions (Hairston, 1988a), expanding the facilities for family visiting (Bloom & Cohen, 1981), increasing funds for visitor agencies (Bloom & Cohen, 1981), and using more community-based alternatives (Fishman & Cassin, 1981).

COMMUNITY-BASED ALTERNATIVES

The 1990 Blue Ribbon Commission on Inmate Population Management focused in its *Final Report* on the need for alternatives to incarceration. The urgency to establish alternatives is the result of a burgeoning and overcrowded prison system. In the 1980s, California witnessed the most dramatic increase in prison population ever experienced in the nation. The population grew from 22,500 in 1979 to 86,000 in 1989. In a decade, there was an increase of over 268 percent in the number of adult prisoners. There are over 110,000 prisoners in 1995. California has relied upon incarceration over probation alternatives, passing more mandatory sentences and sentence enhancements due to a "get tough on crime" political stance. California also returns more parole violators to prison than other states. There were 1,011 parole violators in 1978, compared with 39,976 in 1989. This 1989 figure contrasts with 33,235 returned parolees for the rest of the *entire* country! Obviously, this has been a huge contributor to prison overcrowding in California.

The Blue Ribbon Commission members believe that intermediate sanctions for nonviolent offenders should include the following: electronic monitoring, house arrest, intensive probation and parole supervision, specialized parole and probation caseloads, work furlough, community service victim restitution centers and programs, community detention options, residential and nonresidential substance abuse treatment programs, and other community-based programs in both the private and public sectors. They recommend that the governor adopt a Community Corrections Act to develop these alternatives.

It is important to realize how significant these recommendations are. Most prisoners are nonviolent offenders, and many would be eligible for the alternative options. Of current prisoners, 43 percent committed violent offenses, 27 percent committed property offenses, and 24 percent are serving sentences for drug offenses. The community-based programs could provide benefits to these offenders, particularly when so many are substance abusers (even if their crime was not directly a drug offense). Substance abuse programs are essential.

Second, keeping nonviolent offenders in the community allows them to maintain their family ties and would eliminate the impact of incarceration on the families. Granted, increased community help would be needed for families of offenders participating in these community-based programs, but the majority of the issues raised in this research could be dramatically alleviated. The prisons would be better able to handle visitors if the prison populations were reduced.

Of interest as well is how community programs compare with what is being offered in California prisons. According to the *Final Report*, in 1989, 57,500 prisoners were in some kind of program. Most (26,000) had some type of job at the prison; 7,000 worked in the prison industries; 6,250 were in vocational education programs; 5,600 were participating in full-time academic education programs; 250 were in apprenticeship programs; only 100 were in the sex offender treatment program; 3,300 went to Alcoholics Anonymous or Narcotics Anonymous; and 9,000 participated in programs such as Arts-in-Corrections or had M-2 sponsors. Other than work or education, few rehabilitation programs exist. Significantly, thousands of prisoners fail to participate in any programming.

According to Petersilia (1989), nationwide, fewer than 10 percent of offenders in alternative programs committed new crimes (which were mostly misdemeanors), compared with about 50 percent of regular prisoners on probation or regularly released prisoners. Alternative programs cost less and do a better job of reducing crime.

THE BUDGET

The main driver of what goes on with the CDC is the budget. Youth and Adult Corrections accounted for about 8 percent of general fund expenditures in California for fiscal year 1995–96. That translated to about $3.4 billion, the CDC getting 90 percent of it. Some money for corrections-related operations comes from other sources, so the amount needed is actually higher. California has undertaken the most ambitious prison-building program in the country, with 30 prisons in 1995 and the goal of 40 by the year 2000. The number of staff employed by the CDC stands at 42,412 today in 1995, while in 1989 there were 25,000 budgeted positions.

The amount of money spent on incarcerating people is staggering. The average yearly cost of locking up a person in California is $20,927. In spite of locking up over 110,000 people, the crime rate has not fallen. In spite of our "tough on crime" action, a two-year follow-up study of parolees released in 1992 revealed a recidivism rate of 52.8 percent in 1994. This is a dismal failure; the current practices are not working to make us safer.

The money spent by the CDC goes primarily to operations, staff salaries, and building prisons. Too small a fraction of the money is being spent on programs for prisoners. All signs point to the urgent need to reevaluate our budgetary priorities and our sentencing alternatives.

A SAFETY AND SECURITY MANDATE VS. A PRO-VISITING POLICY

Visiting programs are vulnerable to squeezing and trimming. In 1978–79, rehabilitation was removed from the mission of the criminal justice system, and punishment was acknowledged. According to W. Anderson (interview, May 30, 1991), family support needs to be organized outside of the criminal justice system. Corrections can encourage visiting, but it is not responsible for what happens with families of prisoners. The system is not equipped to deal with families and their problems; it is not in their mission to do so.

Is the mandate of the criminal justice system—to provide safety and security for the public—incompatible with a pro-visiting policy? The system believes it is. It cannot be sensitive to visitors' claims of harassment, for example, when it feels it must do car searches, and strip searches or use metal detectors to keep out contraband. The view is that if the visitors are innocent, they should not feel offended; after all, it is the visitors' well-being that is being protected. But the wives feel that the prison policies punish them for wanting to visit their husbands and maintain their marital ties (Fishman, 1990). They feel their overall treatment is demeaning and has little to do with safety and security. Wright (1973) reminds us that prisons function through punishments to establish a system of control. Many of the punishments to control prisoners are losses of privileges related to their families—loss of visiting, family visits, phone calls, or packages.

I don't believe these views can be successfully reconciled. The experience of the two factions are similar to the oppressor and the oppressed, where the power balance is lopsided. The guard in a uniform, doing his or her job, who has the power to exclude a visitor based on clothing, or who looks down on the prisoner's wife, is not likely to understand the anxiety of that wife as to whether something may go wrong with the visit, how tired she is from driving five or six hours to visit, or the overall fear she feels that her husband may not be safe inside the prison. While prisons may provide a certain degree of law and order, they do not provide justice or compassion. Irwin states, "we need not punish above and beyond imprisonment. . . . We need not and must not degrade, provoke, nor excessively deprive the human beings whom we have placed in prison" (1980, p. 248).

Prisoners' families sharply feel the injustice of the system, from the interaction with lawyers, to the disproportionately minority and poor prison population, to the contempt with which prisoners and their families are treated. Until the system changes philosophically to incorporate the alternatives to incarceration and to move back to a rehabilitation stance that includes acknowledgment of community, families will continue to feel humiliated. Mustin (1988) feels that families of offenders must become an organized constituency to lobby elected officials, to push for these changes. Nazeeh (interview, April 5, 1991) feels that the women don't get the recognition they deserve for their role in prisoner rehabilitation because they are a population hidden from the public. Yet they have the strength to organize their lives, to get to the prison despite obstacles, and to maintain the family structure.

Wives and families of prisoners are a valuable resource for the prisoners, the community, and the nation. You cannot force a person to rehabilitate, but the strongest appeal you can make to an individual is through their intimate bonds and their primary group. The people they care about and who care about them are important. There is no policy more decent and more basic than validating the ties and the roles we hold as human beings. We must find a way to meet the challenge of behavior that is not acceptable in society and must be punished as we simultaneously nurture and support the fundamental structure in society—the family.

Chapter 10

Wives as Caretakers:
There's More to It than That

Examining the daily lives of these women and how they are affected by the prison system brings out three major themes. These themes inform our understanding of women's roles in society as well as the relations of ruling.

First we see that these women may be degraded for their association with prisoners, but they do fulfill the socialized female role of caretaker. Second, given their gender, class, and race locations, their life chances would not be much better if they weren't married to these men. And third, their coping mechanisms and strategies are largely successful. They stand up to an oppressive structure in spite of the hardships. We will examine each of these in greater depth.

Hancock (1989, p. 68) writes: "Whereas the subject of the male statement is apparently *I*, that of the female narrative is consistently *we*." With this focus, women attempt to please those around them, even to the point of not being true to their own feelings. Gilligan (1982, p. 17) states that "Women not only define themselves in a context of human relationships, but also judge themselves in terms of their ability to care." When a prisoner's wife strives to help her incarcerated husband maintain some semblance of husband/father roles, she is simultaneously retaining her role as wife. A prisoner's wife who stands by her man is fulfilling her role as a caretaker. In spite of the fact that society devalues the marriage to a prisoner, and the wife is deprived of the desired couple orientation in her daily life, these wives have attached themselves to the status of their caretaking roles within a marriage. They succeed in the conventionally defined female role.

The result of such socialization has not necessarily been positive for women. Miller (1986, p. 89) says, "when women act on the basis of this underlying psychological motive, they are usually led into subservience." The caretaking role is generally of a subservient affiliation. On a similar note, MacKinnon (1989, p. 51) writes: "Perhaps women value care because men have valued women according to the care they give them. . . . Perhaps women think in relational terms because women's social existence is defined in relation to men."

That women are expected to be family-oriented caretakers while men are not, is reflected in how little attention has been paid to incarcerated men and their roles as fathers, as well as how few studies have been done regarding the male prisoner's relationship with his family from his vantage point. Gender role expectations have influenced this subject bias. We see the emphasis on women and families (studies of wives of prisoners and incarcerated women and their children), not on men and families. The generalized effect of gender socialization brings us to the question of whether women can combine family and a career, while that question is never asked of men. We are socialized in such a way that caring is a gender-related behavior.

It means something very different to be a wife than to be a husband. The caretaking role is a very powerful behavioral and psychological motive. It is a factor that extends beyond whether the woman is married to a prisoner or not. Feminism helps to raise the question of women's place in society and points out the inequities between women and men. Choices and constraints can be examined.

The lives of prisoners' wives cannot be looked at separately from the issues of social power and social structure. The relations of ruling organize gender relations as they do all other institutional aspects—along patriarchal lines (D. E. Smith, 1987). Women's lives, Smith maintains, are determined by forces external to them. This is not to say that women have no choices, but that even women with choices are exploited and discriminated against (hooks, 1984). Like Smith, hooks stresses that the focus must be on systems of domination, not on "men as the enemy." She states that sexism is the practice of domination most people experience, whether as oppressor or oppressed: "It is the practice of domination most people are socialized to accept before they even know that other forms of group oppression exist" (1984, p. 35). Male domination must be put in the context of hierarchical structures, and it is this power orientation that must be changed.

Faludi (1991) points to the unequal status of women in our society. She cites the following statistics: Women are two-thirds of all poor adults. They are more likely then men to live in poor housing, and to have no health insurance, and are twice as likely to draw no pension. Nearly 80 percent of working women are in traditional female jobs, with the worst pay, few chances of advancement, and few or no benefits. A female college graduate still earns less than a male high school graduate. The government doesn't offer family leave or child care programs, and more than 99 percent of private employers do not offer child care. Three-fourths of all high schools violate the federal law banning sex discrimination in education, and women receive less financial aid than men do in college. According to Faludi, women still do 70 percent of the housework.

As women, these prisoners' wives are constrained by multiple factors. It isn't only that they have attached themselves to low-status men (they are still men, nonetheless), but also that on their own, they would most likely be working class with low status. The class issue is fundamental to the criminal justice system in regard to the race and class composition of its male targets. For women, it is both in connection with this system and outside of this system that they will be in a position of discrimination, for as women they are targets of sexism.

Prisons house predominantly poor and working-class prisoners. They are the people with the fewest resources, facing a system that demands lawyers, bail money, time and money for visiting, and so forth. Of course, without money, men and women cannot beat this system. Families become further impoverished because scarce resources must flow to the incarcerated men.

Due to the stigma of imprisonment, the wife may lose her job. She has already lost the financial contribution of her imprisoned husband. She may decide to go on welfare to be able to visit every day and maintain her family contact. She may move closer to the prison, located in a remote part of the state where the economy is depressed and jobs are scarce. Lacking money for a good lawyer, her husband must rely on an overburdened court-appointed public defender, which makes a conviction and longer sentence more likely. And racism is a determining factor in corrections. Seventy percent of the CDC population was nonwhite in 1989, while nonwhites comprised only 40 percent of the population in California. Corrections policy is one aspect of white domination of minorities (Blue Ribbon Commission on Inmate Population Management, 1990).

Most of the women married to prisoners are in the same social class as their husbands. In this study, the wives tended to be better educated. However, this advantage was either insignificant due to the burden of incarceration or it simply enabled some wives to cope more easily. It did not alter their basic experience. The opportunity structure for women is clearly limited. And while we can say that the lives of these prisoners' wives could be different if they had married other men or remained single, that isn't to say their lives would be better. They are blocked by the lack of women in positions of power, by the attitudes in society that women aren't as capable as men, and by policies that treat women and their concerns as secondary. Internalized low expectations function to keep women from achieving their fullest potential. And while many wives become more self-confident and independent while handling the family alone during the period of incarceration, their goal is still getting the husband home to fulfill his male role.

The extreme social control of the prison setting is similar to the controlling nature of other bureaucracies that deal primarily with women. The clearest example is the welfare system, which stigmatizes the recipient and adversely affects self-esteem. Since a man must be absent from the house in order for a woman to receive Aid to Families with Dependent Children, the shame is double—the lack of a man *and* low income. Wives of prisoners face the loss of a man, the stigma of his incarceration, and often, low income.

Repeatedly I found that the type of crime husbands committed was less important to the wives than the fact that incarceration resulted and the man was absent. Their lives revolved around coping with this absence. For many women this meant leading a secret life, hiding all or part of their lives from others. The formal stigma was felt with actual arrest, trial, and imprisonment, while the informal stigma was felt in the loss of respect and family role imbalance. Many women hid the incarceration from family and friends, and some even from their children.

It was impossible for these women to live a normal life because women take on the status of the men in their lives. Male dominance is so deeply ingrained in our society that women are blocked by both their internalized oppression and the relations of ruling—structural blocks to education, jobs, and political power.

While I wouldn't call the wives feminists, they are not the opposite of feminists. Their life position is unique, and how they handle it is worth our attention. I am reminded of Stack's 1974 study, *All Our Kin*, in which she examined survival and coping in a low-income neighborhood. Poverty, racism, welfare regulations, few resources and opportunities—all had powerful impacts on the relationships between men and women. For the men, unemployment was the most important factor in interpersonal relationships. It not only meant the men could not continue their role as economic supporter of their families, but their self-esteem and independence suffered. It was the women who maintained the family through networks of cooperation and obligation with friends and kin. They traded goods, and child care, and swapped resources. While the women coped, their lives were constrained by race, sex, and class. They were unable to eliminate these stresses that permeated their everyday existence.

The prisoners' wives are not passive victims; rather, they are very strong women. In addition to being caretakers (the traditional role for women), they are also survivors of economic hardship, criminal justice stigma, and, in many cases, racism. Their personal relationships are lopsided because the husbands can rarely give any financial support to the family. It is the wives who bring the resources to the prison while they attempt to help the husbands retain some semblance of father/husband roles. However, as with Stack's women, coping does not eliminate the structural stresses of their lives.

What looks to the outsider like an outrageous situation (the wives should obviously leave their prisoner husbands), looks different to the wives. They are standing up to a power structure that most of us never deal with. It is the prisoners' wives who know of the injustices and speak out—even if only among themselves—of the inhumanity of prisons. They, as Gilligan (1990, p. 502) writes, "know what they know and are willing to speak of it." Their lives become a form of political resistance. They are outraged by their experience, and while most of society denounces them and their husbands, the wives condemn the system of oppression that has overtaken their personal lives. It is a system that, for example, introduced a bill (SB 1382) during the 1992 California legislative session to prohibit prisoners on death row and prisoners who have been sentenced to life without the possibility of parole from receiving family visits (the bill did not pass.) Who is being punished here? The wives and families know—while the public never gives it a thought.

Still, as these wives stand up to this power structure, there are obvious limitations. One is that there is an utter lack of support for these families from the public at large. This derives primarily from the fact that their husbands committed crimes and the public is furious. Further, they stigmatize the wives due to guilt by association and the desire to deny human needs and emotions connected with the prisoners. No one could *possibly* love *these* men.

Second, these are women speaking out against injustice and they are not taken seriously. They are speaking out against a sexist system that is also racist and classist, and the prejudices are deeply ingrained in our attitudes, laws, and institutional practices. To alter the experience of wives of prisoners would mean altering the understanding and organization of social resources and social power. It would require a democratization of power and decision-making, as well as the dismantling of sexism. Rather than the victims being stigmatized, responsibility would have to shift to institutions that perpetuate inequality.

Feminism helps us to look at these women's lives from their perspective. The prison system and the wives have different needs and different understandings of these men (prisoner to one, husband/father to the other). From their different perspectives, they are caught up in a web of interlocking institutional constraints and public demands.

Dilorio (1982, p. 14), studying working-class women in automotive van clubs, questioned the value of raising the consciousness of these women who had few economic alternatives to marriage for survival. What could be gained, she wondered, by telling them of the injustices of their personal relationships. Yet I believe that the prisoners' wives I met felt the injustices of the criminal justice system and knew the limitations of their personal relationships in a way that spoke beyond their oppression. They knew they were oppressed and stigmatized, and still they organized to sustain their families and to survive, and beyond that to challenge prison policies and individual guard behaviors. As D. E. Smith (1987) reminds us, by listening to the voices of women who have not yet spoken up, who have a different experience of the world, we will have a continual opening up in our understanding of the social world.

Their survival should spark our consciences to organize *with them*—not us to change them, but to let their experience inform us of what we need to change in the relations of ruling. This glimpse into women's lives as wives of prisoners shows us women's positions in society. We clearly see that in spite of the powerful primary relationship maintenance that women do, women's contributions are devalued. Caring behavior in and of itself is not negative. It is the gender association with women as subservient that devalues it. As long as traits are gender typed, and women are labeled as the lower-status gender, qualities considered feminine and women's ideas will be devalued. If we want these wives to be taken seriously, then caring behavior must be gender neutral. Examining the impact of imprisonment on families demonstrates the impact of gender socialization on family roles and points to the need to examine the intersection of sex, race, and class. These structural constraints must be challenged. We have much to learn from these women, and our challenge is to change together.

Appendix A

Questionnaire

I conducted interviews in person (except for one by mail) in an open-ended question format.

INTRODUCTORY STATEMENT

The purpose of this study is to see how incarceration of a husband or lover affects the legally innocent wife/partner and family. I am interested in how things have changed since incarceration, what's changed for the better, and what's changed for the worse. Policy makers seem to be ignorant that the prison system affects more than those prisoners they are designed to house. The public remains totally unaware of many aspects of the impact of incarceration upon prisoners or their families.

DEMOGRAPHICS (YOURS AND YOUR HUSBAND'S)

Name, age, race, religion, education. About husband: conviction, sentence length, how long he has already served. A short personal history of your relationship (when met, when married, etc.) How often do you visit? How often do you talk on the telephone? How often do you write letters to each other? Do you have family visits?

ECONOMIC IMPACT

Housing: What was your living situation before, and what is it now?
Job: Were you working before? Are you working now? If he added to your

support, what was he doing, and how has his absence affected your financial situation? How has his incarceration affected how you spend your money? Are you receiving social services? Do you need social service assistance?

CHILDREN

How many children do you have, what ages, boys or girls? How has his absence affected the children? Do you have child care problems?

SUPPORT NETWORK

How did your family and friends react when your husband went to prison? Do you have support now of family? Of friends? Is there a way your husband could be more helpful to you in coping with his incarceration? Can you tell others (work, people you meet) about your husband being in prison, or do you live a partly secret life? How do you explain his absence? Do you experience (or have you in the past experienced) social stigma from your husband being in prison? Have your children experienced any problems due to their father being in prison?

RELATIONSHIP ISSUES

What in your relationship has changed for the better? What has changed for the worse? Do you share outside problems, pressures, and decisions with your husband? Does he share what he goes through with you? Would you talk about issues of loneliness and of sexual frustration you experience due to the separation, and how this has affected you? How are your family visits? How do you think you'll cope with the rest of his sentence? What are your dreams and hopes for the future when you are united?

DEALING WITH THE PRISON SYSTEM

What was your experience like with lawyers? How are you affected by the prison system? The guards? Rules? Counselors? How do you feel in the visiting room, before, during and after a visit? Do you have any fears about your husband being in prison, for his health, his safety? Do you worry that he'll be transferred? Do you have any stories or experiences you want to relate?

REHABILITATION

What do you think the prison system could do differently to rehabilitate the prisoners? How do you feel the prison system could strengthen family ties and help maintain family stability? In general, how do you see the role of the family in parole success? How do you see your role in your husband's reintegration? What are your primary concerns regarding your husband's release and reintegration into society? How do you think we can change the public's stereotype of prisoners? If you could tell policy makers your main concerns, what do you think they need to understand? What would you say?

Thank you. Please let me know if your husband is transferred from Soledad, if he is released from prison, or if you move. You will hear from me in four months, when I send the first follow-up questionnaire.

Appendix B

Follow-up Survey Summary

I attempted to follow the women for a period of one year from the date of our interview at four-months, eight-months and one-year. I was able to follow only 13 of the 25 for the full year. Four of the women broke up with their husbands, one of them after his release. Interestingly, he was the only husband to be released whose wife kept in touch with me. Fourteen out of 25 men were transferred.

Within four months of the interviews, women reported these changes: less visiting due to husband being transferred further away, losing a job and getting a new one, giving birth to a baby son, moving, a car accident, waiting to hear from the courts, death in the family, surgery, and no changes. One wife wrote: "[There's] a significant amount of [expense] to travel further and obtain lodging while there. Also due to distance and cost, a decrease in the amount of times I can visit. This is not fair!"

After eight months, women reported a new job, job loss, waiting to hear from the courts, waiting for release or transfer, one woman joined the army, financial problems, not able to visit, no changes, and happier. Said one wife:

With finances slim, the only changes have been less visiting, which can be depressing. But on a lighter note, we have gotten notice he has gotten approval for transfer to Solano, which will be super as far as traveling and being able to see each other more often. It seems by not seeing each other more often than we do, things seem different sometimes—strained, distant. But I guess that is to be expected. We have a family visit March tenth, which will help a bunch. (Vicky)

A year after the interview, women were having difficulty visiting due to transfers and additional distance and cost, one had a court hearing that cut a year off a sentence, several were awaiting release, others felt their marriages were strengthening, they were coping, one was expecting a baby, one had an illness,

and others reported no changes. One women reflected:

This past year has been a good one, one of personal growth and strength for us both. Our unity is also growing. I have no easy answer for a good marriage, but flexibility is important; rolling with the waves is, too. It's all priorities, not getting upset over little things the system does to us. (Pat)

Follow-up Survey Results

Name	4 Month Transferred	4 Month Released	8 Month Transferred	8 Month Released	12 Month Transferred	12 Month Released
Terri	Vacaville-South		No	No	No	No
Tijuan	San Quentin		No	No	No Response	
Isabel	No	No	They broke up			
Cynthia	No Response					
Jeni	No	No	No	No	Vacaville-South	
Minerva	No	No	No	No	Soledad-Central	
Cyndi	San Quentin	Tracy	No	No	No	No
Cathy	Monterey County Jail		No Response			
Marie	No Response (they broke up)					
Valerie	No Response (they broke up)					
Sue	No	No	No	No	No	No
Laura	No	No	No	No	No	No
Colleen	No Response		No	No	No Response	
Carrie	No	No	No	No	No Response	No
Sharon	San Quentin	No	No	No	No	No
Jean		Yes (then they broke up)				
Janet	Vacaville-South		No	No	San Quentin	
Wanda	Vacaville-South		No	No	No Response	
JoAnna	No Response					
Marilyn	No	No	No	No	Vacaville-South	
Vicky	No	No	No	No	Vacaville-South	
Misty	Tracy	No Response				
Betty	No	No	San Luis Obispo	No	No	No
Pat	No	No	No	No	No	No
Charlene	San Quentin	No	No	No	No	No

Note: "Transferred" means the prisoner was sent to another prison; "Released" means the prisoner completed his sentence and was released from prison.

Appendix C

The Author on Her Research Experience

I did not become the wife of a prisoner in order to do this study. Rather, once I found myself in this other world, the idea grew and grew in my mind to speak out about how women associated with prisoners were treated and what we went through. While we women were somewhat different from each other, we shared an intense bond due to our common circumstance. I was probably more like these women than Whyte was in his Italian neighborhood (*Street Corner Society*, 1955) or Liebow was in an all-black neighborhood in *Tally's Corner* (1967). I was, however, more white, more middle-class, and more educated than most prisoners' wives. But I never felt like a stranger, except perhaps with the monolingual Spanish-speaking women. Being a women and being a prisoner's wife were the overriding traits for acceptance. As I felt accepted by the women, so I accepted them unconditionally.

My marriage significantly affected every aspect of my life outside of the prison. How I spent my time was oriented around visiting days or writing letters on days I did not visit. When planning my budget, I looked at money for gas, motels, and vending machines or set aside money to send packages or for food for family visiting. Not being with my husband meant nights alone, time spent in social situations as a single person, and living where many people did not know I was married. I spent many nights crying, and I spent a great deal of time daydreaming.

While I did not experience everything some of my interviewees did, the prison context sets itself up as an "us versus them" environment. There is outright oppression, arbitrary rules, and fear of reprisal. There is a constant sense of a great wrong being committed—*by the system*—, and that "only if people knew," this wouldn't be tolerated. Many of the women had never been involved with the criminal justice system, and were absolutely shocked at what they now encountered on a daily or weekly basis. I had been in jail several times for political protests and also had read a great deal about prisons as a sociologist, so my shock wasn't how things were done but how it affected my entire life to love someone in prison.

My field notes reflect a constant state of exhaustion after visiting, as well as other physical side effects: headaches and stomachaches. The visiting room was very uncomfortable—too hot or too cold, very smoky from cigarettes—and, being a vegetarian, I couldn't eat much from the vending machines. The physical space affected me negatively; this made it difficult, because I had to go there to see my husband.

I experienced many fog counts, when I would have to wait until they re-counted all the men due to heavy fog and the increased risk of escape. On one visit, I arrived at the prison at 8 A.M. and didn't get to see my husband until 11:30 A.M. These waits are very hard on visitors, especially as we were not allowed to wait indoors. During lockdowns, visiting was slowed because the guards had to escort prisoners into the visiting room one at a time rather than page them and have them walk across the yard on their own. There were long delays on many occasions.

The guards had a big impact on my visits. Their attitudes could make a visit pleasant or nerve-wracking. The "good" guards didn't monitor our behavior or walk around. Others watched like hawks and made the atmosphere tense. We were told, as other couples were told, to keep moving if we leaned against the wall, or to stop hugging or kissing. Granted, some couples acted outrageously: couples snuck behind the vending machines and had sex, or prisoners stole the vending machine money box. These actions are resented by visitors and other prisoners since our visits could be terminated due to such misconduct. I had a generally pleasant relationship with some officers—one even was interested in this research. But mostly the guards were a sore spot to everyone. It would be difficult for it to be otherwise, given what they represent.

I felt as other wives did that family visiting—that time when you get two nights with your husband—was wonderful, but also very difficult. The first family visit I had was a shock because the physical conditions were like a slum. The trailer area was deplorable, the interior was dirty, curtains were ripped, furniture was dirty and stained, and there were cockroaches. It was very uncomfortable and hard to relax. Since I was grateful for the privacy, I felt I had to swallow some of my pride.

Along with the shared physical spaces, I shared the issue of secrecy with the other wives. That was a very uncomfortable way to live. I told some people, such as family and some friends, but not employers or acquaintances. I did have some rejection from family and friends, and that was painful. There is no question that wives of prisoners are stigmatized. People believe prisoners are very lowly, and are not sympathetic to them or their families.

Other experiences I had include having my letters to my husband read by guards and the lack of privacy to deal with relationship problems. During stressful times, my husband would tell me how he would hear from others information about me that had been in letters. Another time we faced the disappointing news that an appeal had been denied, but could not really comfort one another. We also could not argue in the visiting room, since couples try not to air their personal lives in front of others. These restrictions on private life have an impact on your relationship. But the reality was that whenever people did get loud, argue, or cry, they would become the object of attention and gossip.

I did not want to write an autobiography, so I have focused on what the other wives experienced. But my experiences were also so similar to those of most of the women, that this study is very close to my story. My life was easier than most, since I did not have children, I had a job, I had a car, and my drive to the prison was only two hours each way.

Reinharz (1979) writes that experiential epistemology allows the researcher to come to terms with her own experiences through self and group reflection. Certainly the process of dialoging with the other wives in the course of this work helped me make sense of my own feelings. Another part of this experience is that my husband was an informant for me. In the course of getting to know him and about his reality, I learned about other people. There were things I learned through my husband about the husbands of the women I interviewed that the women themselves might not have known.

The women were very excited about the research and often asked me how it was going. I felt an enormous obligation to them to complete the research and to let the world know what was happening to them. I believed it was extremely important for their words to be heard.

There were many reschedulings and cancellations of interviews. That was very frustrating. On two occasions I drove to other cities for interviews and the wives had forgotten about them (one was not at home, the other I tracked down at another house). I could not always confirm the interviews because not all wives had telephones. On the other hand, some interviews occurred spontaneously, after visiting hours. I would get excited by the pace of interviews, then frustrated by cancellations and no-shows.

I would sometimes give other wives rides home, saving them bus fare and long waits. I tried not to do this if it would be out of my way, since I was very tired by visiting. However, these rides were always filled with animated conversation and were enjoyable.

I was offered drugs during one interview, and simply declined. I was in many homes and met many family members. I became very fond of these women from hearing so many moving stories, sharing their struggles, and marveling at their persistence. When talking with them, except for the unusual content of the conversation, I felt very normal. I believe this is a story that deserves to be told, that people should understand the impact of the prison system on families and attempt to humanize that system.

Participant observation is unequaled as a research method in its access to the inner lives of participants. I feel it allows a greater grasp of the subjects' experiences and a better opportunity for the researcher to understand her own experience and views. It does require an openness and flexibility on the part of the researcher to let in experiences different from her own. I am certain that a women not married to a prisoner could not have grasped as fully how life felt to these wives. As painful as my experience was, I am grateful for it and for what we — wives and husbands — shared.

References

Acker, J.; Barry, K.; & Esseveld, J. (1991). Objectivity and truth: Problems in doing feminist research. In M. M. Fonow & J. A. Cook (Eds.), *Beyond methodology* (pp. 133–153). Bloomington: Indiana University Press.

Adams, D., & Fischer, J. (1976). The effects of prison residents' community contacts on recidivism rates. *Corrective and Social Psychiatry and Journal of Behavioral Technology, Methods, and Therapy, 22,* 21–27.

Anderson, G. M. (1985, October 26). The uncertain relationship: Families of prisoners. *America,* 257–260.

Anderson, K.; Armitage, S.; Jack, D.; & Wittner, J. (1990). Beginning where we are: Feminist methodology in oral history. In J. M. Nielsen (Ed.), *Feminist research methods* (pp. 94–112). Boulder, CO : Westview Press.

Arendell, T. (1986). *Mothers and divorce: Legal, economic, and social dilemmas.* Berkeley: University of California Press.

Barry, E. (1985a, March–April). Children of prisoners: Punishing the innocent. *Youth Law News,* 12–15, 18.

———. (1985b, July–August). Reunification difficult for incarcerated parents and their children. *Youth Law News,* 14–16.

Becker, H. S. (1963). *Outsiders: Studies in the sociology of deviance.* New York: Free Press.

Belle, D. (1982). The stress of caring: Women as providers of social support. In L. Goldberger & S. Breznitz (Eds.), *Handbook of stress: Theoretical and clinical aspects* (pp. 496–503). New York: The Free Press.

Bem, S. (1974). The measurement of psychological androgyny. *Journal of Consulting and Clinical Psychology, 42,* 155–162.

Bernard, J. (1981). *The female world.* New York: Free Press.

Bloom, B., & Cohen, M. (1981). *Marriage in prison: An exploratory study.* Unpublished manuscript, San Francisco State University, Department of Social Work.

Blue Ribbon Commission on Inmate Population Management. (1990). *Final report.* Sacramento, CA: Prison Industry Authority.

Blume, E. S. (1990). *Secret survivors: Uncovering incest and its aftereffects in women.* New York: John Wiley & Sons.

Boynton, K. R., & Pearce, W. B. (1978). Personal transitions and interpersonal communication among submariners' wives. In E. J. Hunter & D. S. Nice (Eds.), *Military families: Adaptation to change* (pp. 130–141). New York: Praeger.

Brodsky, S. L. (1975). *Families and friends of men in prison: The uncertain relationship.* Lexington, MA: Lexington Books.

Broverman, I. K.; Vogel, S. R.; Broverman, D. M.; Clarkson, R.E.; & Rosenkrantz, P. S. (1972). Sex-role stereotypes: A current appraisal. *Journal of Social Issues, 28* (2), 59–78.

Brown, G.; Bhrolchain, M.; & Harris, T. (1975). Social class and psychiatric disturbance among women in an urban population. *Sociology, 9,* 225–254.

Bunch, C. (1979). Not by degrees. *Quest, 5* (1), 7–18.

Bureau of Justice Statistics. (1991). *Women in prison.* Special Report. Washington, DC: U.S. Government Printing Office, U.S. Department of Justice, Office of Justice Programs.

Burstein, J. (1977). *Conjugal visits in prison.* Lexington, MA: Lexington Books.

Cannon, L. W.; Higginbotham, E.; & Leung, M. L. A. (1991). Race and class bias in qualitative research on women. In M. M. Fonow & J. A. Cook (Eds.), *Beyond methodology* (pp. 107–118). Bloomington: Indiana University Press.

Carlson, B. E., & Cervera, N. J. (1991). Incarceration, coping, and support. *Social Work, 36* (4), 279–285.

Chodorow, N. (1978). *The reproduction of motherhood.* Berkeley: University of California Press.

Comiskey, P. (1989, January). About visiting. *The California Prisoner, 6.*

Daniel, S. W., & Barrett, C. J. (1981). The needs of prisoners' wives: A challenge for mental health professionals. *Community Mental Health Journal, 17,* 310–322.

deBeauvoir, S. (1952). *The second sex.* New York: Vintage Books.

Dill, D., & Feld, E. (1982). The challenge of coping. In D. Belle (Ed.), *Lives in stress: Women and depression.* Beverly Hills, CA: Sage.

Dilorio, J. A. (1982). *Feminist fieldwork in a masculinist setting: Personal problems and methodological issues.* Paper presented at the North Central Sociological Association Annual Meetings, Detroit.

Dvorchak, R. (1991, June 30). Many vets' marriages are casualties of war. *San Jose Mercury News,* 19A.

Eagly, A. H. (1987). *Sex differences in social behavior: A social role interpretation.* Hillsdale, NJ: Lawrence Erlbaum Associates.

Epps, E. (1982). *Law breaking and peacemaking.* Argenta, BC, Canada: Argenta Friends Press.

Faludi, S. (1991). *Backlash: The undeclared war against American women.* New York: Crown Publishers.

Family and Corrections Network. (1986). Policy recommendations on families of adult offenders. *Proceedings of the First National Leadership Conference on Families of Adult Offenders.* Waynesboro, VA.

Fee, E. (1983). Women's natural and scientific objectivity. In M. Lowe & R. Hubbard (Eds.), *Woman's nature: Rationalizations of inequality* (pp. 9–25). New York: Pergamon Press.

Feinman, C. (1983). Historical overview of the treatment of incarcerated women—myths and realities of rehabilitation. *The Prison Journal, 63* (2), 12–26.

Fishman, L. T. (1990). *Women at the wall.* Albany: State University of New York Press.

Fishman, S. H., & Cassin, C. J. (1981). *Services for families of offenders: An overview.* Washington, DC: National Institute of Justice.

Flanagan, R., & Jamieson, K. (1988). *Sourcebook of criminal justice statistics 1987.* Washington, DC: U.S. Government Printing Office, Department of Justice, Bureau of Justice Statistics.

Fonow, M. M, & Cook, J. A. (Eds.). (1991). *Beyond methodology: Feminist scholarship as lived research.* Bloomington: Indiana University Press.

Fox, G. L. (1981). Family and the ex-offender: Potentials for rehabilitation. In S. E. Martin et al. (Eds.), *New directions in the rehabilitation of criminal offenders* (pp. 406–423). Washington, DC: National Academy Press.

Freeman, J. (1975). *The politics of women's liberation.* New York: David McKay.

French, M. (1985). *Beyond power: On women, men, and morals.* New York: Ballantine Books.

Friedman, S., & Esselstyn, T. C. (1965). The adjustment of children of jail inmates. *Federal Probation, 29,* 55–59.

Furstenberg, F., & Nord, C. (1982, April). *The life course of children of divorce: Marital disruption and parental contact.* Paper presented at the annual meeting of the Population Association of America, San Diego.

Gilligan, C. (1982). *In a different voice.* Cambridge, MA: Harvard University Press.

———. (1990). Joining the resistance: Psychology, politics, girls and women. *Michigan Quarterly Review, 29* (4), 501–536.

Glaser, D. (1964). *The effectiveness of a prison and parole system.* New York: Bobbs-Merrill.

Goetting, A. (1982a). Conjugal association in prison: Issues and perspectives. *Crime and Delinquency, 28* (1), 52–71.

———. (1982b). Conjugal association in prison—the debate and its resolution. *New England Journal on Prison Law, 8* (1), 141–154.

Goffman, E. (1963). *Stigma: Notes on the management of spoiled identity.* Englewood Cliffs, NJ: Prentice-Hall.

Goode, W. J. (1956). *After divorce.* Glencoe: Free Press.

Governor's Advocacy Council on Children and Youth. (1981, June). *Women, families and prison.* Raleigh: North Carolina Department of Administration.

Graham, H. (1983). Caring: A labour of love. In J. Finch & D. Groves (Eds.), *A labour of love: Women, work and caring* (pp. 13–30). Boston: Routledge and Kegan Paul.

Hairston, C. F. (1988a). Family ties during imprisonment: Do they influence future criminal activity? *Federal Probation, 52* (1), 48–52.

———. (1988b). Fathers in prison: Not just convicts. *Nurturing Today, 10* (1), 40–41.

Hancock, E. (1989). *The girl within.* New York: Fawcett Columbine.

Hart, C. (1993, Summer). Family visiting common in U.S. *The California Prisoner,* 8.

Hartman, L., & Cronk, D. (1988). *Doing life and hard time.* Unpublished manuscript, California State University, Hayward.

Hartsock, N. C. M. (1979). Feminist theory and the development of revolutionary strategy. In Z. R. Eisenstein (Ed.), *Capitalist patriarchy and the case for socialist feminism* (pp. 56–77). New York: Monthly Review Press.

———. (1983). The feminist standpoint: Developing the ground for a specifically feminist historical materialism. In S. Harding & M. B. Hintikka (Eds.), *Discovering reality* (pp. 283–310). Dordrecht, Netherlands: D. Reidel.

Hays, W. C., & Mindel, C. H. (1973). Extended kinship relations in black and white families. *Journal of Marriage and the Family, 35,* 51–57.

Hedin, T. (1986, December 15). My husband is in prison. *Newsweek,* 14.

Henriques, Z. W. (1982). *Imprisoned mothers and their children.* Washington, DC: University Press of America.

Hill, R. (1949). *Families under stress: Adjustment to the crisis of war separation and reunion.* New York: Harper & Brothers.

Hinds, L. S. (1980). *The impact of incarceration on low-income families.* Washington, DC: Community Services Administration.

Hochschild, A. (1989). *The second shift.* New York: Avon Books.

Holt, N., & Miller, D. (1972). *Explorations in inmate-family relationships.* Research Report no. 46. Sacramento: California Department of Corrections.

hooks, b. (1984). *Feminist theory: From margin to center.* Boston: South End Press.

Howe, F. (1979). Sexual stereotypes start early. In P. I. Rose (Ed.), *Socialization and the life cycle* (pp. 52–63). New York: St. Martin's Press.

Howser, J. F., & MacDonald, D. (1982, August). Maintaining family ties. *Corrections Today,* 96–98.

Hughes, E. C. (1945). Dilemmas and contradictions of status. *American Journal of Sociology, 50,* 353359.

Hurst, J. (1983, April 17). Prison marriages are no honeymoon. *Los Angeles Times,* 1, 3, 34.

Irwin, J. (1980). *Prisons in turmoil.* Boston: Little, Brown.

Jones, A. (1980). *Women who kill.* New York: Fawcett Crest.

Kaplan, B. H.; Cassell, J. C.; & Gore, S. (1977). Social support and health. *Medical Care, 15* (5), 46–58.

Keve, P. W. (1974). *Prison life and human worth.* Minneapolis: University of Minnesota Press.

Koban, L. A. (1983). Parents in prison—comparative analysis of effects of incarceration on families of men and women. *Research in Law, Deviance and*

Social Control, 5, 171–183.

Koenig, C. (1985). *Life on the outside: A report on the experiences of the families of offenders from the perspective of the wives of offenders.* Chilliwack, B.C.: Community Services, Correctional Service of Canada—Pacific Region.

Lake, A. (1973, October). The revolt of the company wife. *McCall's,* 22–32.

LeClair, D. P. (1978). Home furlough program effects on rates of recidivism. *Criminal Justice and Behavior, 5* (3), 249–259.

———. (1985). *The effect of community reintegration on rates of recidivism: A statistical overview of data for the years 1971 through 1982.* Boston: Massachusetts Department of Corrections.

Lester, H. (1982). The special needs of the female alcoholic. *Social Casework, 63,* 451–456.

Liebow, E. (1967). *Tally's corner: A study of negro streetcorner men.* Boston: Little, Brown.

Lowenstein, A. (1986). Temporary single parenthood—the case of prisoners' families. *Family Relations, 35,* 79–85.

MacDonald, D. G. (1980). *Follow-up survey of post-release criminal behavior of participants in family reunion program.* Washington, DC: U.S. Department of Justice.

MacKinnon, C. A. (1989). *Toward a feminist theory of the state.* Cambridge, MA: Harvard University Press.

McCubbin, H. I., & Dahl, B. B. (1976). Prolonged family separation in the military: A longitudinal study. In H. I. McCubbin, B. B. Dahl, & E. J. Hunter (Eds.), *Families in the military system* (pp. 112–144). Beverly Hills, CA: Sage.

Miller, J. B. (1986). *Toward a new psychology of women.* Boston: Beacon Press.

Millman, M., & Kanter, R. (1975). *Another voice: Feminist perspectives on social life and social science.* Garden City, NY: Anchor Books.

Moffitt, P. F.; Spence, N. D.; & Goldney, R. D. (1986). Mental health in marriage: The roles of need for affiliation, sensitivity to rejection, and other factors. *Journal of Clinical Psychology, 42* (1), 68–76.

Morris, P. (1965). *Prisoners and their families.* London: George Allen & Unwin.

———. (1967). Fathers in prison. *British Journal of Criminology, 7,* 424–430.

Mosher, H. E. (1954, November 8). Mrs. All America: Football wives. *Newsweek,* 56–57.

Mustin, J. W. (1988). The family: A critical factor for corrections. *Nurturing Today, 10* (1), 6–7.

New York State Defenders Association. (1985, May). *What prisons do to people.* Albany: New York State Defenders Association.

Nielsen, J. M. (Ed.). (1990). *Feminist research methods: Exemplary readings in the social sciences.* Boulder, CO : Westview Press.

Oakley, A. (1974a). *Woman's work: The housewife, past and present.* New York: Pantheon Books.

———. (1974b). *Sociology of housework.* London: Martin Robertson.

———. (1981). Interviewing women: A contradiction in terms. In H. Roberts (Ed.), *Doing feminist research* (pp. 30–61). Boston: Routledge & Kegan Paul.

Ohlin, L. E. (1954). *The stability and validity of parole experience tables*. Doctoral dissertation, University of Chicago.

Oliver, J. (1983). The caring wife. In J. Finch & D. Groves (Eds.), *A labour of love: Women, work and caring* (pp. 73–83). Boston: Routledge and Kegan Paul.

Petersilia, J. (1989). Criminals should be given alternatives to prison. In D. L. Bender & B. Leone (Eds.), *Crime and criminals: Opposing viewpoints* (pp. 70–74). San Diego: Greenhaven Press.

Pleck, J. (1979). Men's 'family work role': Three perspectives and some new data. *Family Coordinator, 28*, 481–488.

Reinharz, S. (1979). *On becoming a social scientist*. San Francisco: Jossey-Bass.

Rich, A. (1986). *Of woman born: Motherhood as experience and institution*. New York: W.W. Norton.

Rienerth, J. G. (1978). Separation and female centeredness in the military family. In E. J. Hunter & D. S. Nice (Eds.), *Military families: Adaptation to change* (pp. 169–184). New York: Praeger.

Rollo, N. (1988, January 8). *Maintaining personal ties between prisoners and their loved ones*. Dallas: OPEN. (Cassette recording).

Rollo, N., & Adams, L. W. (1987). *Keeping it together: Social and psychological adjustments of offenders and their loved ones*. Dallas: OPEN.

Rolls, J. A. (1989, November 18). *The recovering female alcoholic: A family affair*. Paper presented at the 75th annual Speech Communication Association Convention, San Francisco.

Rosenfeld, J. M., & Rosenstein, E. (1973). Towards a conceptual framework for the study of parent-absent families. *Journal of Marriage and the Family, 35* (1), 131–135.

Rosenfeld, J. M.; Rosenstein, E.; & Raab, M. (1973). Sailor families: The nature and effects of one kind of father absence. *Child Welfare, 52*, 33–44.

Schneller, D. P. (1976). *The prisoner's family: A study of the effects of imprisonment on the families of prisoners*. San Francisco: R and E Research Associates.

Schwartz, M. C., & Weintraub, J. F. (1974). The prisoner's wife: A study in crisis. *Federal Probation, 38*, 20–27.

Seidenberg, R. (1974, February 18). An expert talks about problems of executive wives. *U.S. News and World Report*, 80–83.

Shanley, M. L., & Schuck, V. (1975, December). In search of political woman. *Social Science Quarterly, 55*, 632–644.

Sheehy, G. (1979). The urge to merge. In P. I. Rose (Ed.), *Socialization and the life cycle* (pp. 97–107). New York: St. Martin's Press.

Showalter, D., & Jones, C. W. (1980). Marital and family counseling in prisons. *Social Work, 25* (3), 224–228.

Smith, D. E. (1987). *The everyday world as problematic: A feminist sociology*. Boston: Northeastern University Press.

Smith, L. (1987, March 25). The waiting years. *Sacramento Bee*, AA1–AA4.

Sommers, T., & Shields, L. (1987). *Women take care*. Gainesville, FL: Triad.

Spanier, G. B., & Casto, R. F. (1979). Adjustment to separation and divorce: An analysis of 50 case studies. *Journal of Divorce, 2*, 241–253.

Stack, C. B. (1974). *All our kin: Strategies for survival in a black community.* New York: Harper & Row.

Stanton, A. M. (1980). *When mothers go to jail.* Lexington, MA: Lexington Books.

Steese, E. (1988, April 28). Wives of locked up husbands. *Christian Science Monitor,* 23.

Swan, L. A. (1981). *Families of black prisoners: Survival and progress.* Boston: G. K. Hall .

Taylor, V., & Rupp, L. J. (1991). Researching the women's movement. In M. M. Fonow & J. A. Cook (Eds.), *Beyond methodology* (pp. 119–132). Bloomington: Indiana University Press.

Toth, L. (1985, July). Prison life: Notes from a survivor. *The California Prisoner,* 9.

Vaughan, D. (1986). *Uncoupling: How relationships come apart.* New York: Vintage Books.

Vaux, A. (1985). Variations in social support associated with gender, ethnicity, and age. *Journal of Social Issues, 41*, 89–110.

Velimesis, M. L. (1969). Criminal justice for the female offender. *American Association of University Women, Journal, 63* (1), 13–16.

Wallerstein, J. S. & Kelly, J. B. (1980). *Surviving the breakup: How children and parents cope with divorce.* New York: Basic Books.

Weinstein, C. (1989, August). Sick call. *The California Prisoner,* 11.

Weiss, R. S. (1974a). The provisions of social relationships. In Z. Rubin (Ed.), *Doing unto others* (pp. 18–24). Englewood Cliffs, NJ: Prentice-Hall.

———. (1974b). *Loneliness: The experience of emotional and social isolation.* Cambridge, MA: MIT Press.

———. (1979). *Going it alone: The family life and social situation of the single parent.* New York: Basic Books.

Weitzman, L. J. (1985). *The divorce revolution: The unexpected social and economic consequences for women and children in America.* New York: Free Press.

Wells, M. (1974, January 18). Thrice I cried, or, how to be a minister's wife if you loathe it. *Christianity Today,* 7–10.

Westkott, M. (1990). Feminist criticism of the social sciences. In J. M. Nielsen (Ed.), *Feminist research methods* (pp. 58–68). Boulder, CO : Westview Press.

Whyte, W. H. (1951, October). The wives of management. *Fortune,* 86–88, 204–213.

———. (1955). *Street corner society: The social structure of an Italian slum.* Chicago: University of Chicago Press.

Wilson, C. (1980). The family. In Camberwell Council on Alcoholism, *Women and alcohol.* New York: Tavistock.

Wiseman, J. P. (1980). The "home treatment": The first steps in trying to cope with an alcoholic husband. *Family Relations, 29* (4), 541–549.

Wright, E. O. (1973). *The Politics of Punishment.* New York: Harper & Row.

Wylie, M. S. (1988, September/October). Around the network. *Networker*, 12–14.

Zalba, S. (1964). *Women prisoners and their families*. Children of Women Prisoners Project. Sacramento: California Department of Social Welfare Department of Corrections.

Zur-Szpiro, S., & Longfellow, C. (1982). Fathers' support to mothers and children. In D. Belle (Ed.), *Lives in stress: Women and depression* (pp. 145-153). Beverly Hills, CA: Sage.

Index

About the Author

LORI B. GIRSHICK is on the faculty of Warren Wilson College, where she teaches sociology and women's studies courses. She has experience in the domestic violence field and has worked in an agency providing services to people with HIV. Dr. Girshick's work has appeared in *The Prison Journal, Reproductive Health Resources, Violence Update, Policy Studies Journal,* and *Policy Issues for the Elderly Poor.*

ISBN 0-275-95409-9

90000>

9 780275 954093

EAN

HARDCOVER BAR CODE